£22.50

PATTERN GRADING FOR
MEN'S CLOTHES

Other books on clothing from Blackwell Scientific Publications

Pattern Grading for Women's Clothes
Gerry Cooklin
0 632 02295 7

Pattern Grading for Children's Clothes
Gerry Cooklin
0 632 02612 X

Introduction to Clothing Manufacture
Gerry Cooklin
0 632 02661 8

The Technology of Clothing Manufacture
Harold Carr and Barbara Latham
0 632 02193 4

Introduction to Clothing Production Management
A.J. Chuter
0 632 01827 5

Knitted Clothing Technology
Terry Brackenbury
0 632 02807 6

Fashion Design and Product Development
Harold Carr and John Pomeroy
0 632 02893 9

Materials Management in Clothing Production
David J. Tyler
0 632 02896 3

PATTERN GRADING FOR MEN'S CLOTHES

The Technology of Sizing

GERRY COOKLIN

OXFORD

BLACKWELL SCIENTIFIC PUBLICATIONS

LONDON EDINBURGH BOSTON

MELBOURNE PARIS BERLIN VIENNA

© Gerry Cooklin 1992

Blackwell Scientific Publications
Editorial offices:
Osney Mead, Oxford OX2 0EL
25 John Street, London WC1N 2BL
23 Ainslie Place, Edinburgh EH3 6AJ
3 Cambridge Center, Cambridge,
    Massachusetts 02142, USA
54 University Street, Carlton
    Victoria 3053, Australia

Other Editorial Offices:
Librairie Arnette SA
2, rue Casimir-Delavigne
75006 Paris
France

Blackwell Wissenschafts-Verlag
Meinekestrasse 4
D-1000 Berlin 15
Germany

Blackwell MZV
Feldgasse 13
A-1238 Wien
Austria

First published 1992

Set by Best-set Typesetter Ltd.
Printed and bound in Great Britain by
The Alden Press, Oxford

DISTRIBUTORS

Marston Book Services Ltd
PO Box 87
Oxford OX2 0DT
(*Orders:* Tel: 0865 791155
          Fax: 0865 791927
          Telex: 837515)

USA
Blackwell Scientific Publications, Inc.
3 Cambridge Center
Cambridge, MA 02142
(*Orders:* Tel: 800 759-6102
          617 225-0401)

Canada
Oxford University Press
70 Wynford Drive
Don Mills
Ontario M3C 1J9
(*Orders:* Tel: 416 441-2941)

Australia
Blackwell Scientific Publications
(Australia) Pty Ltd
54 University Street
Carlton, Victoria 3053
(*Orders:* Tel: 03 347-0300)

British Library
Cataloguing in Publication Data
Cooklin, Gerry
    Pattern grading for men's clothes: the technology
    of sizing.
    I. Title
    646.4072

ISBN 0-632-03305-3

Library of Congress
Cataloging in Publication Data
Cooklin, Gerry.
    Pattern grading for men's clothes: the technology of sizing /
    by Gerry Cooklin.
        p.   cm.
    Includes bibliographical references.
    ISBN 0-632-03305-3
    1. Tailoring – Pattern design.   2. Clothing and dress
    measurements.   I. Title.
TT590.C69   1992
646.4'072 – dc20   91-46456

This book is dedicated to Chaim Pollak, the late Managing Director of Bagir Ltd, of Israel and England. It was my privilege to work with him for twelve years.

Contents

viii

Preface

During the past twenty years or so, the styling of men's clothes has drastically moved away from the uniformity which had dominated menswear for nearly a century. While there is still a demand for classic look garments, fashion has become an integral element in clothing for men of all ages.

The same changes have occurred in pattern grading. Today, the variety of garment types, the dynamics of fashion and the multiplicity of domestic and overseas size ranges demand a far more flexible approach to the entire subject of sizing. Gone are the days of rigid, rote-like pattern construction methods and mechanistic grading. Instead, the grading of each new style requires a high degree of technical versatility combined with a practical understanding of accurate sizing and the maintenance of design proportions.

It is my sincere hope that this book will help the student and the professional to increase their perception of what is really involved in the grading of garment patterns for the new look male.

Finally, I should like to express my very grateful thanks to my colleagues at Bagir in Israel and England and to many friends in the industry and retailing who most generously gave me all the benefits of their knowledge and experience.

Gerry Cooklin

Acknowledgements

My thanks to the following suppliers and agents who kindly gave their permission to reproduce the photographs in Chapters 3, 7, 9 and 24.

Assyst	Munich	Germany
Berliner Buestenfabrik	Berlin	Germany
Cybrid Ltd	Manchester	England
Design Center	Tel-Aviv	Israel
Durkopp-Adler	Beilefeld	Germany
Gerber Inc.	Connecticut	USA
Lectra Systemes	Bordeaux	France
Morplan	London	England
Schön	Pirmasens	Germany
Neel Agencies	Tel-Aviv	Israel
Ormi Ltd	Tel-Aviv	Israel
Stacy Enterprises	Ra'anana	Israel
Technotex	Tel-Aviv	Israel

PART 1

INTRODUCTION

Chapter 1

Then and Now

The history of the men's clothing industry goes back a very long time, and from about the middle of the 16th century books on pattern construction started appearing in European languages. Grading as a technique was virtually unknown because men's garments were cut to individual measurements and the construction systems provided scales of proportions for the body and limbs according to the chest girth and height.

Although today these systems might seem very primitive, the tailors of those times knew a great deal about sizing and proportions and the cutting of garments for all types of body figurations. They were also helped by the fact that during the making up of the garments, they used manipulatory techniques such as shrinking and stretching to create fitting effects which the pattern construction systems could not provide. A tailor would be given only the basic components of a garment by the cutter and would be expected to know how to cut linings, body interlinings and collars, etc. In addition, the cutters played it safe by providing seam inlays in every conceivable direction.

From about the middle of the 19th century, ready made garments were based on a very simple sizing system. There were three main sizes – small, medium and large – and as the pattern construction systems of that time equated girth with height, the ready made clothing shops had to maintain alteration departments. The first ready made garments were far from being ready to wear for most men. Also about this time, the prototype of today's three piece suit became the accepted form of masculine dress and this basic form remained static for about 100 years.

In the 1960s, London's Carnaby Street became the centre for what was to be called the 'Mod' look and from that time onward, fashion entered the realm of men's clothing. While the freer and more informal styling of men's garments was mainly directed towards the younger generation, it also influenced the concept of what was considered to be the classic look for mature men. These changes were not as dramatic and frequent as those fashions for young men, but they were pronounced enough to gradually make the male public more fashion conscious. This new consciousness, coupled with new types of garments, laid the foundations for the men's clothing industry of today.

Since the heyday of Carnaby street, new and more rational pattern construction systems have been developed and, more importantly, the necessity for accurate sizing systems has become recognised in order to provide better sizing quality and to maximise expensive selling space by closing or drastically reducing the alteration departments.

Today, there is no doubt that for the large majority of men mass produced garments are really ready to wear and some of the reasons for this are examined in the next chapter.

Chapter 2

Sizing Systems

In comparison to women's wear, the commercial sizing systems for men's clothing offer a far wider range of fittings, not only in height groups but also in body form. For women's garments there are usually three height groups – short, medium and tall – and two fitting groups – regular and outsize – with the outsize fittings mostly confined to the medium height group.

As against this, one of the largest retailers of menswear in Europe regularly stocks six categories of fittings, each in one or two height groups. Table 2.1 shows the choice of fittings and height groups available for one chest girth.

Needless to say, the variety of garments available in each fitting and height category would be commensurate with the market size for each particular combination.

While not every retailer of men's outerwear carries such an extensive range of fitting possibilities, it is an established fact that as regards sizing, the majority of men can purchase off-the-peg clothes with a very high standard of fitting quality. Where does it all start?

Again, in comparison to the sizing systems for women which have been developed from large scale anthropometric surveys, there is very little published scientific data regarding men's sizes and measurements. The major researches into men's sizing have been concentrated on establishing ergonomic data and size charts for the manufacture of military uniforms. While these size charts are very informative, they are limited to a relatively small age group and cannot be used in the wider commercial context. There is, however, an enormous reservoir of knowledge gained from many years of practical experience with men's sizing, and it is this empirical approach which is the dominant factor of commercial sizing systems for men's clothes.

Appendix A contains a number of size charts, some of which have been published by professional organisations or appear in text books, while others have been compiled by leading retailers. What is very noticeable when comparing these size charts is their similarities regarding the characteristics of change in secondary girths and lengths relative to the increase or decrease of chest girth and height. For example, irrespective of whether the chest girth size interval is 4 cm or 5 cm, the across back interval is 25% of this key interval while the shoulder length is consistent at 6% of the same interval. Length grades such as neck to waist

Table 2.1. Fittings and height groups available for chest girth of 100 cm

Fitting	Height	Waist girth (cm)	Seat girth (cm)
Regular	Medium – 177	88	108
Slim	Tall – 186	88	110
Large	Medium – 177	92	110
Athletic	Medium – 177	84	104
Athletic	Tall – 188	84	106
Stocky	Short – 165	94	110
Stocky	Medium – 171	92	108
Portly	Short – 164	104	110
Portly	Medium – 170	104	110

or sleeve length also have this consistency of proportions.

Thus for all practical purposes, these charts in total represent a very accurate picture of the sizing systems currently used, and although actual measurements might differ from chart to chart the proportions of change correspond in many cases.

It is this consistency of proportions which provided the foundation for the grading system demonstrated in this book. The objective was not to compile and publish yet another collection of size charts, but rather to present an accurate and practical concensus in terms of pattern grading, of the sizing systems used by clothing manufacturers and retailers who have a wealth of experience in this subject.

The structure of sizing systems

A sizing system is the term used to describe the total range of size and fitting combinations available in ready made garments. Each system contains a number of size ranges, with each one catering for the sizing requirements of a specific group of the population. Systems can be elaborate, containing many size ranges, or restricted to possibly one or two ranges. As an example, Fig. 2.2 shows the structure of the German

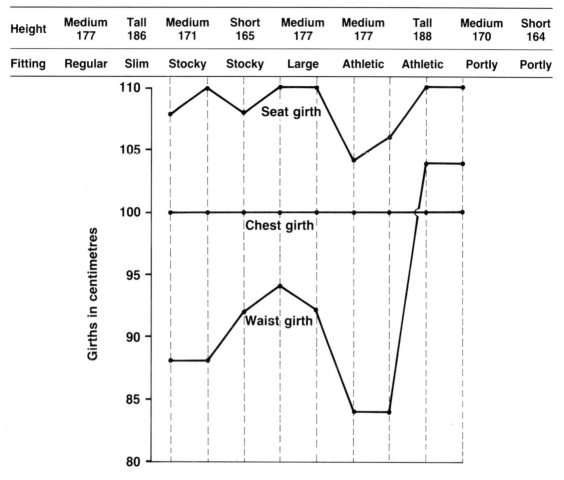

Height	Medium 177	Tall 186	Medium 171	Short 165	Medium 177	Medium 177	Tall 188	Medium 170	Short 164
Fitting	Regular	Slim	Stocky	Stocky	Large	Athletic	Athletic	Portly	Portly

Fig. 2.1. Fitting variations based on one chest girth.

sizing system which is very widely used throughout mainland Europe and Scandinavia.

Up until a few years ago, the number of size ranges available for men in any one country was limited to those ranges considered worth producing by the domestic manufacturers. This picture has drastically changed through the rapid development of the international trade in clothing which, in turn, has increased the profitability of producing speciality size ranges. Thus today the general public can purchase garments which are accurately sized, and not compromise choices of fitting quality.

While the elements of fashion, quality and price influence the type of garments produced in any one size range, the two central components of size ranges are the same for all market sectors: height and fitting.

HEIGHT

There are two aspects to consider:

(1) The general height category such as short, medium or tall (long).
(2) The range of heights covered within the height category and their incremental values from size to size.

All the size charts used as references for the grading system demonstrated in this book displayed the same approach to the question of height: within each size range there are dynamic height grades. Two examples of this structure can be seen in Tables 2.2 and 2.3, which are extracts from size charts used by one of England's largest retailers of men's wear.

These two tables are illustrated graphically in Fig. 2.3, and apart from showing typical examples of the height function in size ranges, the jacket length graph also highlights the overlaps within the system.

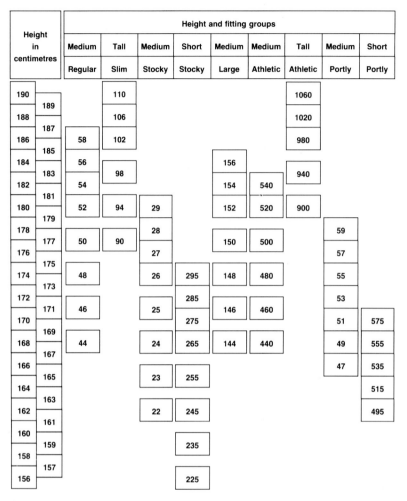

Fig. 2.2. German sizing system and size symbols.

Table 2.2. Men's regular jackets – jacket length

Size	36	38	40	42	44	46
Short	72	73	74	75	76	77
Regular	75	76	77	78	79	80
Tall	79	80	81	82	83	84

FITTING

This is the second component of a size range and is based on the relationships between the measurements of the main girths, especially the relationship between the chest and waist girths. This specific relationship is called the drop and equals one half of the difference between these two girths; it is expressed numerically with a plus or minus value. Table 2.4 gives a small extract from the German HAKA-Verband sizing

Table 2.3. Men's regular trousers – outside leg

Size	28	30	32	34	36	38	40	42
Short	97.0	97.9	98.8	99.7	100.6	101.5	102.4	103.3
Regular	102.6	103.5	104.4	105.3	106.2	107.1	108.0	108.9
Tall	108.8	109.7	110.6	111.5	112.5	113.3	114.2	115.1

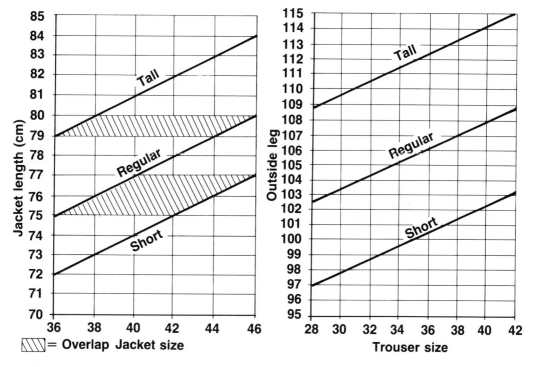

Fig. 2.3. Height groups and garment lengths.

system and shows the drop values according to the two girth measurements for each fitting range.

As regards pattern grading, the factors of height and fitting have the following influence:

- The prime and secondary length grades are dynamic for all height group categories irrespective of fitting. Consequently the techniques of a grading system must incorporate these dynamic aspects simply and accurately.
- While fittings can and do vary within a given size range, these variations cannot effectively be incorporated into a pattern grading system because

Table 2.4. Drop values of two girth measurements for each fitting range

Regular fitting: drop −6 and −5

Size	44	46	48	50	52	54	56
Chest	88	92	96	100	104	108	112
Waist	76	80	84	88	92	98	102

Sizes 44–52 inclusive −12 cm difference. Sizes 54 and 56 −10 cm difference.

Athletic fitting: drop −8

Size	440	460	480	500	520	540
Chest	82	92	96	100	104	108
Waist	72	76	80	84	88	92

A consistent size interval of −16 cm between chest and waist.

Corpulent fitting: progressive drop +2, +3 and +4

Size	47	49	51	53	55	57	59
Chest	92	96	100	104	108	112	116
Waist	96	100	104	110	114	120	124

Sizes 47–49–51 +4 cm difference. Sizes 53–55 +6 cm difference. Sizes 57–59 +8 cm difference.

some of the adjustments required, especially those concerning corpulent fittings, belong to pattern construction which is not a function of pattern grading. Thus the system demonstrated will operate on the basis of a consistent drop for all the sizes being graded.

TO SUM UP

Internationally, the men's clothing industry produces garments in many different size ranges. A grading system, if it is to be efficient, must have the basic foundations which enable it to be applied to any rational size chart. The development of the principles involved in this approach are examined in the next part of this book.

PART 2

SYSTEM DEVELOPMENT

Chapter 3

Measurements

The essential pre-requisite of grading is a size chart that details the combination of measurements which together make up each size. Those used for men's garments can be divided into two categories:

(1) Girth and girth related such as chest girth and across back.
(2) Height and height related, for example back neck to knee and sleeve length. Figs 3.1, 3.2 and 3.3 show the locations of the most usually used measurements. Their definitions are:

Girth and girth related

(1) Chest girth: at the level of the maximum chest girth back and front.
(2) Waist girth: at the average level around the trunk of the natural waist.
(3) Seat girth: at the average seat line level.
(4) Neck girth: the circuit of the neck base starting from the cervical.
(5) Thigh girth: measured at the fork line.
(6) Knee girth: measured at tibial height.
(7) Ankle girth: measured at the level of the ankle bone (talus).
(8) Upper arm girth: at the armscye level of the trunk.
(9) Wrist girth: at the level of the distal end of the ulna.
(10) Across back: horizontally across the back between the posterior (back) armscyes.
(11) Across chest: horizontally across the chest between the anterior (front) armscyes.
(12) Shoulder length: Along the shoulder line from the neck base to the intersection of the armscye and shoulder lines.

Height and height related

(13) Stature: from the vertex of the head, perpendicularly to the floor.
(14) Cervical height: perpendicularly from the cervical to the floor.
(15) Nape to waist line: cervical to natural waist line level at back.

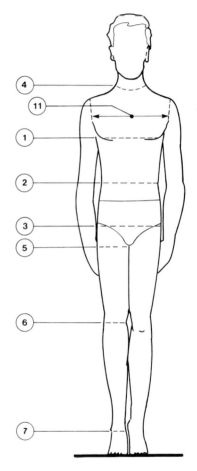

Fig. 3.1. Front view measurements.

(16) Waist line to seat line: between the average waist and seat levels at the side of the body.
(17) Waist line to crutch line (body rise): from the average waist level at the side to the level of the fork.
(18) Crutch line to knee line: at the side, between the fork and knee lines.
(19) Knee line to ankle line: at the side, between the knee and ankle lines.
(20) Outside leg: from the average waist level at the side perpendicularly down to the ankle line.

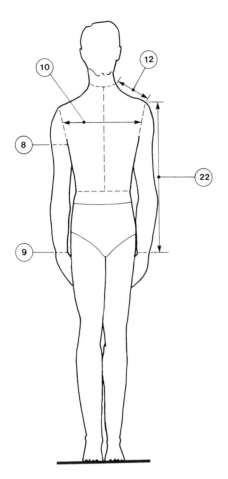

Fig. 3.2. Back view measurements.

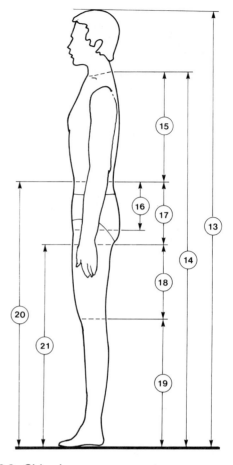

Fig. 3.3. Side view measurements.

(21) Inside leg: from the centre of the fork, perpendicularly down to the ankle line.

(22) Sleeve length: from the vertex of the sleeve head to the wrist line. There are some other methods of measuring sleeve length, but for grading purposes this is the easiest location to work with.

While many designers have traditionally preferred to try garments on live models, the workroom stand is becoming more accepted as a basis for fitting criteria. Fig. 3.4 shows two forms which are widely used in the British and Continental clothing industries.

TO SUM UP

Very few, if any, commercial size charts provide all the measurements listed above, and most professional pattern graders have their own rules for calculating values which are not given in the charts they work from. However, in order that a grading system will produce the best results, it must be capable of generating the values which are not generally given in size charts. It is this detail which makes the difference between a 'just' graded pattern and a well graded pattern.

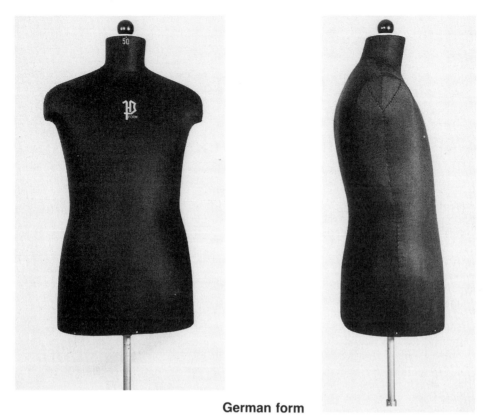

German form

British form

Fig. 3.4. Workroom stand forms.

Chapter 4

The Method of Development

For the development of this grading system, the method used to determine the value of the grading increments was to make a precise analysis of the values provided by the size charts reproduced in Appendix A. The objective was to produce a detailed, overall picture of what these manufacturers and retailers were doing as regards the grading of their garments.

Firstly, two working definitions:

(1) *Size interval*: This refers to the amount by which a specific measurement changes from size to size. For example, Table 4.1 shows that the chest girth size interval for the size range 44–58 is 4 cm.
(2) *Increment*: This is used to describe the amount by which a variable quantity increases or decreases from size to size. An increment can be used on its own, as in the shoulder length grade, or can be a sub-division of a major increment as the shoulder length grade is in the across back or across chest grade.

The methods used for this analysis were:

Girths and girth related

Irrespective of the size interval, all the intervals for girth related measurement values were expressed as a percentage of the chest girth interval. These percentages were then averaged and the results were rounded off when necessary. For example, Table 4.2 shows an extract of the calculations used to determine the value of the across-back grade in relation to the chest girth grade. This, when rounded off to 25%, became the standard factor for determining the across back grade for a given chest girth size interval. This calculation was performed for all the other girth related values for body garments, sleeves and trousers.

Height and height related

A similar method was used for the height related values, with the difference that the actual size intervals were averaged rather than being expressed as a percentage of the height interval. The reason is that with two exceptions, none of the size charts examined provided a height size interval. During the analysis of the height related values, another factor to emerge was

Table 4.1. Chest girth size interval

Size	44	46	48	50	52	54	56	58
Chest girth	88	92	96	100	104	108	112	116

Table 4.2. Calculations for value of across-back grade

Chest girth interval	Across back interval	%
4 cm	10 mm	25
5 cm	12 mm	24
5 cm	12.5 mm ($\frac{1}{2}$ in)	25
4 cm	10 mm	25
5 cm	12 mm	24
5 cm	12.5 mm ($\frac{1}{2}$ in)	25
	Average	24.6%

Table 4.3. Calculation of sleeve length values

	Sleeve length for 5 cm interval mm	Sleeve length for 4 cm interval mm
	—	10
	12	—
	—	10
	12	—
	12	—
	—	10
Average for interval:	12	10

the similarity between the values used for specific chest girth size intervals. In this case it was 4 cm and 5 cm. Table 4.3 shows an example, with the calculation for the sleeve length values and the similarities.

The results of these analyses for body garments, sleeves and trousers are presented in the following two chapters.

Chapter 5

Body Garments, Sleeves and Related Components

The first applications of the analysis are concerned with establishing the locations and functions of the increments required for grading body garments and then extending these to the grading of basic components derived directly from the body.

Each of the increments has its own notation and this nomenclature will be used throughout the book. The reason for using notation is that for each demonstration grade, the increment values will be given for English and Continental sizing systems and these values vary from system to system.

Increments for the girth and girth related grades

NOTATION	LOCATION AND FUNCTION
A	Total pattern width grade from the front edge to the centre back. As the chest, waist and seat girth size intervals are the same, A is equal to one half of the girth size intervals.
B	The total front width grade from the front edge to the centre of the side section. This is the nominal location only of the side seam and the relevance of this will be examined further on.
C	The total back width grade from the centre of side section to the centre back.
D	This is the across-back grade and is located on a line between the centre back and the innermost line of the back armhole.
2E	This is the total grade for the width of the side section, which is located on the chest line between the across back and across chest lines.
E	Half of 2E and is used for side section width and sleeve width grades.
F	The neck base width grade used equally on the front and back for garments with closed necklines such as formal shirts. For garments with open necklines, such as those with lapels, F

becomes a sub-increment of the across chest grade.

G	The front and back shoulder length grade. On the front, G is one of the increments which make up the across chest grade and on the back it is a part of the across back grade.
H	Part of the across chest grade. Used in conjunction with increment F for garments with open necklines and on its own when the garment has a closed neckline.
I	This is the combined value of H + F and is used as one increment for part of the across-chest grade.
J	The total across chest grade on the chestline from the front edge to the armhole.

Figs. 5.1–5.4 relate to the girth grades for the body. Fig. 5.1 shows the basic divisions of width for body garments, front, side and back. As a starting point the side seam is nominally located at the centre of the side section. Fig. 5.2 shows the function of increment E in the conventional placements of the side seam or seams. Fig. 5.3 illustrates the dual function of increment H as a component of the across chest grade. Fig. 5.4 sums up the locations of the basic width grade increments.

Increments for the height related grades

NOTATION	LOCATION AND FUNCTION
K	This increment is for the total length grade of the garment and its value varies according to the length of the garment being graded, i.e. blouson, jacket or overcoat etc.
L	Used for grading the depth of armhole and can be part or all of the neck to waist grade. It is also utilised for grading the crown height of the sleeve.
M	When necessary, this increment is applied between the chest and waist

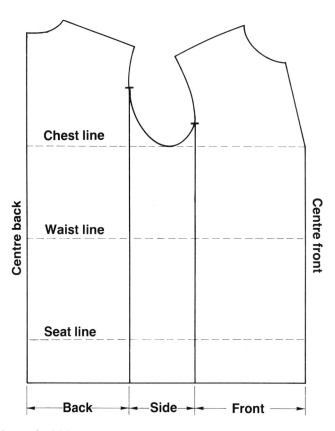

Fig. 5.1. The basic divisions of width.

	lines and it becomes part of the neck to waist length grade.
N	This is the neck to waist grading increment and can be equal to L or the total of L + M.
O	Like K, the value of O would vary according to the garment length but in all cases N + O = K.

The locations of the length grades are shown in Fig. 5.5 and the combined width and length grades are illustrated in Fig. 5.6.

Derived grades for body garments

There are three basic components for body garments whose grades are derived directly from the corresponding parts of the body. The first of these components is the basic one piece sleeve.

The construction of the upper section of an inset sleeve is directly related to the width and depth of the armhole and in order to maintain the constructional relationship between armhole and sleeve, they should both be graded by the same values. Fig. 5.7 shows the derivation of the sleeve grade from that for the armhole. The connections between them are sleeve width and crown height.

SLEEVE WIDTH

The side section of the body in which the armhole is located is graded in its width by the value of 2E, and the same value would apply to the matching under section of the sleeve. As this under section is one half of the sleeve width, the same value of 2E has to be applied to the top half of the sleeve in order to retain the width relationship between the under and top sections.

Thus the application of 2E plus 2E to the sleeve girth at the sleeve head base line effectively divides the sleeve into four sections of width, with each section being graded in the width by increment E. Fig. 5.8 shows these divisions on a one piece sleeve and how the quarter sections are combined to produce the top and under sections of the sleeve.

17

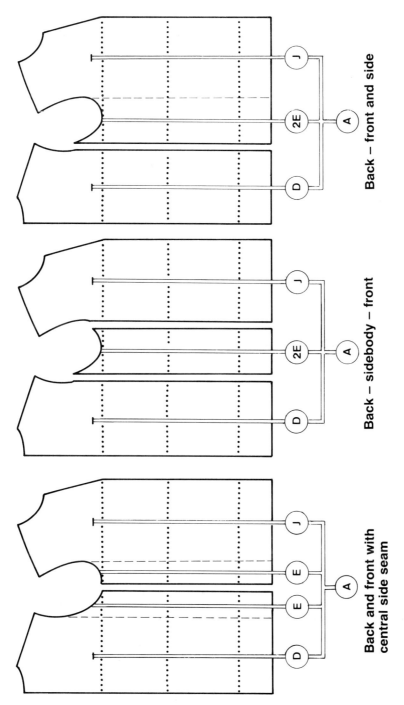

Fig. 5.2. Conventional garment width divisions.

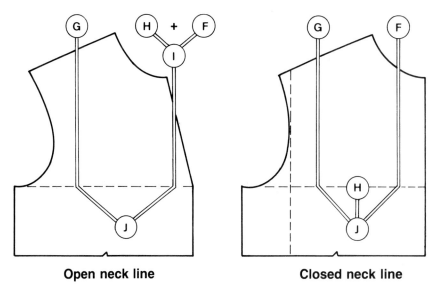

Open neck line   **Closed neck line**

Fig. 5.3. The across chest grades.

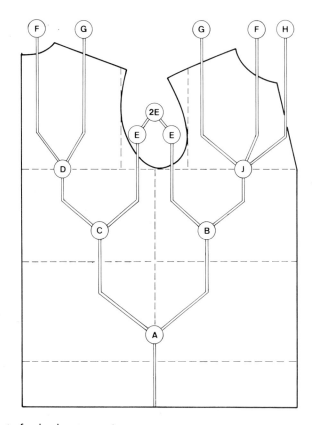

Fig. 5.4. Width increments for body garments.

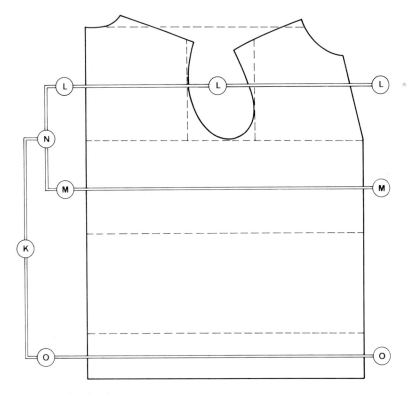

Fig. 5.5. Length increments for body garments.

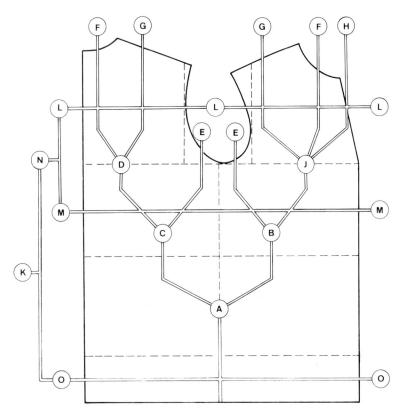

Fig. 5.6. Combined width and length grades for body garments.

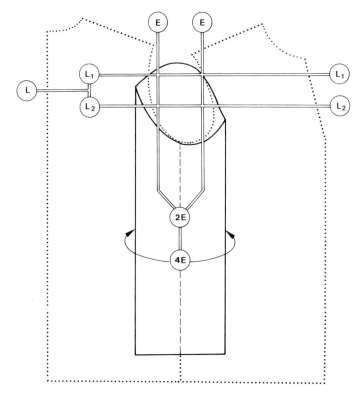

Fig. 5.7. Derivation of sleeve grade.

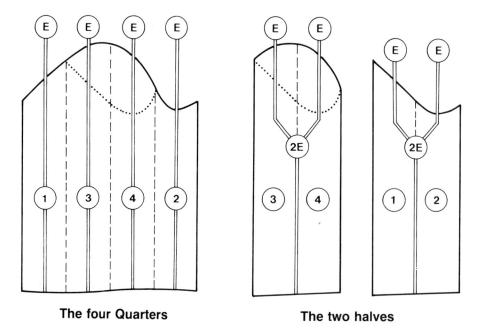

The four Quarters

The two halves

Fig. 5.8. Top and under sections of basic sleeve.

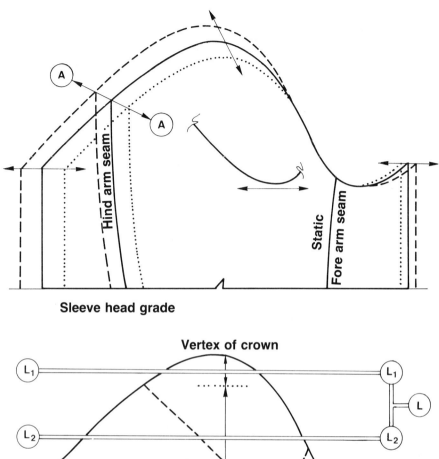

Sleeve head grade

Vertex of crown

L_1 L_1

L

L_2 L_2

Sleeve head base

The division of increment L

Fig. 5.9. Hindarm seam length and the sleeve head grade.

CROWN HEIGHT

This is measured from the base line of the sleeve head to the crown vertex and this distance is graded by the same increment and value as that used to grade the armhole depth. The increment used for both these functions is increment L which can be used in its entirety for the sleeve head or divided into two parts, L1 and L2, when the sleeve has an undersleeve. This is because when the sleeve head is graded in width and

height, the hind arm seam intersects the sleeve head at a different level. Fig. 5.9 (top) illustrates the sleeve head grade and line A-A shows how the level of the intersection point changes from size to size. The locations of L1 and L2 are shown in Fig. 5.9 (bottom) and their values and applications will be given in the demonstration grade for the two-piece tailored sleeve (Chapter 14).

The notation and function of the increments used for the basic one piece sleeve grades are (Fig. 5.10):

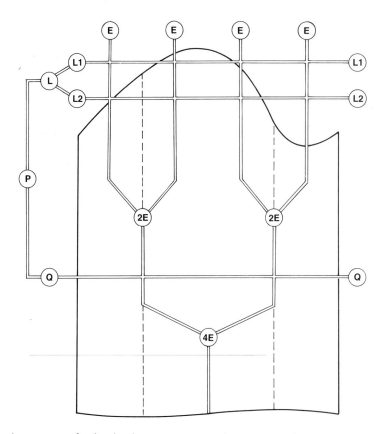

Fig. 5.10. Grading increments for basic sleeve.

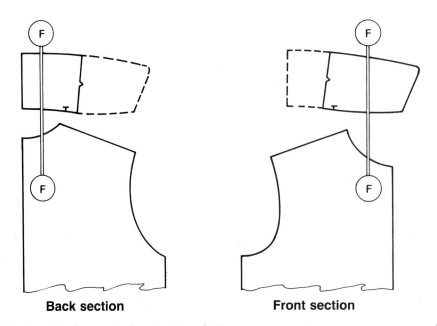

Back section   **Front section**

Fig. 5.11. Derivation of collar grade for closed neck lines.

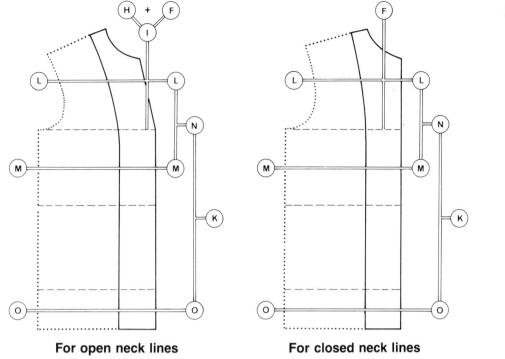

For open neck lines   **For closed neck lines**

Fig. 5.12. Derivation of facing grades.

Table 5.1. Increment table for body garments

Increment	Grading function	Validation	Size interval 4 cm	Size interval 5 cm
A	Half of chest girth size interval	= B + C	20	25
B	Total front width grade from front edge to centre of side section	= E + F + G + H J + E	12.5	16
C	Total back width grade from centre back to centre of side section	= F + G + E A − B	7.5	9
D	Across back	mostly = F + G	5	6
E	Part of side section and sleeves	2E + A − (D + J)	2.5	3
F	Neck base width and collars	—	2.5	3
G	Shoulder length	—	2.5	3
H	Part of across chest	= J − (G + F)	6	7
I	Composite increment	= F + H	7.5	10
J	Across chest	= F + G + H	10	13
K	Full garment length	= N + O	—	—
K	Jacket	= N + O	10	12
K	Knee length	= N + O	15	18
K	Ankle length	= N + O	21	25
L	Depth of armscye and sleeve head	—	5	6
M	Used when N is greater than L	= N − L	—	—
N	Neck to waist	—	5	6
O	Variable length grade	= K − N	—	—
O	Jacket	= K − N	5	6
O	Knee length	= K − N	10	12
O	Ankle length	= K − N	16	19
P	Total sleeve length	= L + Q	10	12
Q	Part of sleeve length	= P − L	5	6

SLEEVES

NOTATION	LOCATION AND FUNCTION
E	Derived from the side section grade for the body and used in a multiple of four to grade the sleeve at the bicep girth line. This increment is also used for grading the cuff circumference of sleeves and this particular function is demonstrated in all the relevant grading examples.
L	Derived from the armhole depth grade and in total is applied between the sleeve head base and its vertex. Fractions of L are also used when necessary.
P	This increment represents the total sleeve length grade from the crown vertex to the cuff line and one of the sub-increments of this increment is increment L.
Q	Another sub-increment of P, applied between the sleeve head base and cuff lines when the total of the sleeve length grade is greater than the value of increment L.

COLLAR

The second derived grade is that of a basic collar for a closed neck line and only increment F is involved. This is the increment used to grade the back and front neck base widths (Fig. 5.11) and the total length grade for a half collar pattern would therefore be equal to 2F. Increment F is also used for the back neck and across chest grades of open neck garments.

FACINGS

The last grade derived directly from the body is for the front edge facing which can have two forms:

(1) An open neck front i.e. having a lapel or waistcoat opening.
(2) A closed neckline such as that for a garment which buttons up to the neck.

For both these facing forms, the same increments are applied as those for the corresponding section of the front; these relationships are shown in Fig. 5.12. There is no practical reason to grade the facing width below the level of the chest line.

Table 5.1 sums up the values of all the increments used for the body and derived grades for 4 cm and 5 cm size intervals, and the calculations used for validating the increment values are also given. The relevant parts of this table are repeated for all the demonstration gradings.

Chapter 6

Trousers

Nearly every size chart examined during the process of developing the grades for trousers worked on three or four height groups. The principle of this sizing system was that the inside leg measurement remained static for all the sizes within the height category but the outside leg length changed through the application of the body rise grade between the crutch and waist lines. Table 6.1, an extract from an English retailer's size chart, shows the principles of this system.

The other size charts showed a dynamic grade for both the inside and outside leg measurements, with the additional length applied between the crutch line and the bottom. Apart from the technique for applying this additional length, the grades for the static and dynamic systems are exactly the same.

The notations, functions and locations of the increments used for the trouser grades are (Fig. 6.1):

NOTATION	LOCATION AND FUNCTION
W	This is the waist girth grade and is equal to a quarter of the size interval for this measurement.
H	The seat girth is graded by this increment whose value is one quarter of the seat girth size interval. As most sizing systems change the waist and seat girths by the same amount from size to size, they have in effect one value.
T	This increment, when added to the seat girth grade of H, becomes the thigh girth grade for each panel. The total grades for the waist and seat girths are spread over four panels,

Table 6.1. Leg measurements for three height groups

Short height

Size	28	30	32	34	36	38	40	42
Inside leg	74	74	74	74	74	74	74	74
Outside leg	96.7	97.6	98.5	99.4	100.3	101.2	102.1	103

Medium height

Size	28	30	32	34	36	38	40	42
Inside leg	79	79	79	79	79	79	79	79
Outside leg	102.3	103.2	104.1	105.0	105.9	106.8	107.7	108.6

Tall height (Long)

Size	28	30	32	34	36	38	40	42
Inside leg	84	84	84	84	84	84	84	84
Outside leg	108.5	109.4	110.3	111.2	112.1	113.0	113.9	114.8

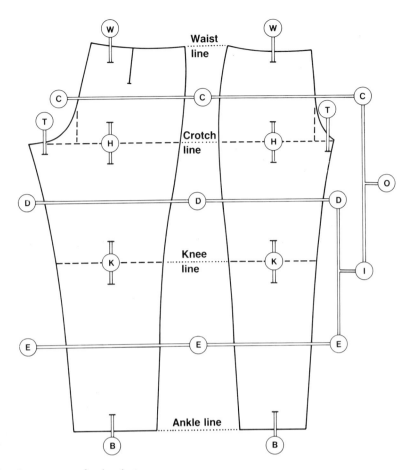

Fig. 6.1. Grading increments for basic trousers.

Table 6.2. Increment table for trousers (increments in millimetres)

Notation	Grading function	Validation	Size interval 4 cm	5 cm
W	One quarter of the waist girth size interval	—	10	12.5
H	One quarter of the seat girth size interval	—	10	12.5
T	A component of the thigh girth size interval	One half of thigh girth = H + T	2	2.5
K	One half of knee girth interval	—	5	6
B	One half of bottom girth interval	—	4	5
C	Body rise	—	7	9
D	Crutch line to knee line	—	2.5	3
E	Knee line to ankle line	—	2.5	3
I	Inside leg	When used I + D + E =	5	6
O	Outside leg	When I is static	7	9
		When I is dynamic, then O = I + C	12	15

NOTATION	LOCATION AND FUNCTION
	while the total grade for the thigh girth is spread over two panels.
K	Applied at the knee line, this increment is equal to one half of the knee girth grade for each leg.
B	For a full length trouser, increment B is applied at the ankle line and is also equal to one half of the bottom grade for each leg.
C	Applied between the crutch and waist lines, this increment grades the body rise. When C is added to T it provides the grade for the back and front rises which are measured from the intersection of the inside leg seams at the crutch line to the waist line at the front or back.
D	This increment is used for dynamic inside and outside leg grades and is applied between the crutch and knee lines. Its main function is to maintain proportions as the leg section length changes.
E	Also used for dynamic inside and outside leg grades and has the same function as increment D. It is applied between the knee and ankle lines.
I	This is the total of D plus E when they are used, and is in effect the inside leg length grade. For static length, inside leg grades D, E and I are not required.
O	The outside leg length grade of O is measured on the side seam from the waist line to the ankle line. The value of this increment can change by C only from size to size, or by the combined value of C plus I.

Table 6.2 sums up the values of all the increments used for the trouser grades for the 4 cm and 5 cm size intervals and the calculations for validating the increment values. The relevant parts of this table are repeated for all the trouser grade demonstration gradings.

Where all the relevant measurements are provided by the size chart being used, the increment values can be calculated from the chart. Where some required size intervals are not given, the values under the size interval heading can be used.

TO SUM UP

As mentioned previously, the increment values given in Tables 5.1 and 6.2 represent a practical consensus of the size charts referred to during the development of the system demonstrated in this book. It is possible that other size charts could produce different values from those shown in the tables, but this is not the real crux of the matter. The point is to know the relationships between measurements and increments, how to validate the values of increments and how and where to apply them. There is no one best way for all grades, any more than there is one provenly best system for sizing men's clothing.

PART 3

GRADING APPLICATIONS

Chapter 7

The Set-Ups

Manual pattern grading has four stages:

(1) The preparation for grading
(2) Grading the patterns
(3) Checking the grades
(4) Completing the graded patterns

To develop a systematic and efficient method of working, the routines within each stage should be followed closely. The applications of these routines are demonstrated throughout the examples in this book and after some practice with the essentials of the system, short cuts can be developed in the light of individual experience of working to specific grading requirements.

Preparation

This is the first stage concerned with all the preparatory work before the actual grading is performed. It consists of the following routines:

AXES

Pattern grading is a technique which in effect reproduces the construction of an original pattern in another size. It follows, therefore, that this reconstruction process should be based on the same construction lines as those which were used for the original pattern.

Most conventional pattern construction systems are based on a regular, four-sided shape divided lengthways and widthways by lines running at right angles to each other (Fig. 7.1). These lines are used to derive the axes of movement for pattern components. The axes themselves can be on a parallel to the CB or CF or any one of the major girth lines.

During grading there are two principal axes of movement for patterns, along the X and Y axes where the actual direction of movement is relative to the intersection of these two axes (Fig. 7.2). As these axes are at right angles to each other, the pattern construction lines are adhered to and alignment in both directions is maintained throughout the grading. Fig.

7.3 shows some examples of the typical positioning of the main axes for body garments and they all have a direct relationship to the lines which were used for originally drafting the patterns. With the exception of bias cuts, the grain line of patterns provides a good reference for the X axis, from which the Y axis can be derived.

Without exception, the X and Y axes must always be marked on the base size pattern before starting any other preparatory work.

SECONDARY AXES

Apart from the X and Y axes, secondary axes are also needed, especially in connection with the length grades. A typical body garment could have up to three length grades using:

• Increment L for the armhole depth grade.
• Increment L for the waist line to chest line grade.
• Increment O for the balance of the garment length.

When required, these secondary axes are marked on the paper parallel to the Y axis; according to the number and value of the grading increment used, there are three methods which can be employed (Fig. 7.4):

Method 1 Where increment M is not incorporated into the grade and the values of increments L and O are exactly the same, the axes for these grades have a dual purpose. This means that one set of secondary axes can be used for two sizes which are to be graded by the same interval, up and down from the base size.

Method 2 In the event that the value of increment L is less than that of increment O, each size would require the marking of individual secondary axes.

Method 3 When increment M is incorporated into the grade, the marking of secondary axes is required for each size. Dual purpose axes can only be utilised when:

• Increment O = increment M
or
• Increment O = increment M plus increment L.

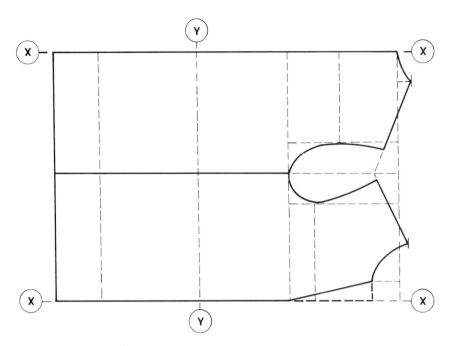

Fig. 7.1. Pattern construction and grading axes.

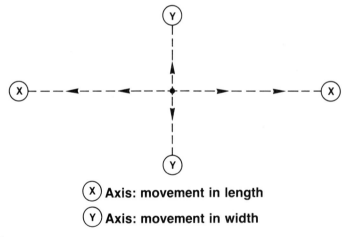

(X) **Axis: movement in length**

(Y) **Axis: movement in width**

Fig. 7.2. The axes of movement.

To prevent confusion when using a number of secondary axes, it is recommended that each set be marked in a different colour.

The marking of secondary axes is the second routine in the preparation stage.

ORIGIN POINTS

These are the points from which the width grades start and they are mostly located at the intersection of a

pattern line and the Y axis. Fig. 7.5 shows two typical examples of the positions of origin points, and all the up and down width grade increments are measured from this point. Origin points are not necessarily located at the intersection of the X and Y axes.

ORIGIN LINES (Fig. 7.6)

This refers to a pattern line and/or axis which will be common to all the sizes graded for a particular

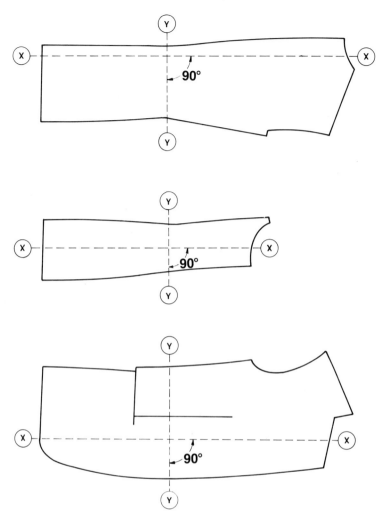

Fig. 7.3. Positions of grading axes for body garments.

component. These origin lines can be of two types, internal and external.

Internal origin lines are used when the width grades for each size are made in two directions from the common origin. Trouser leg grades are a typical example of the use of an internal origin line, which in Fig. 7.6 is the X axis.

External origin lines are the most frequently used method where one edge of a pattern is common to all the sizes graded for the component. External origin lines also make checking simpler because the total width grades can easily be seen in comparison with one and another.

The locations of origin lines are a matter of choice and convenience because their position does not affect the final results of the grades. In practice, a pattern can be graded from any selected origin line although it is

preferable to work from a location where all the pattern movements for the width grade of one size are in one direction only from the origin line.

INCREMENTS (Fig. 7.7)

At the start of all of the demonstration gradings in this book there is a diagram of the component to be graded together with the positions of the grading increments to be used. Also shown is a table which gives the values of the increments, in millimetres, for each of the two size intervals.

According to the chosen interval, the secondary axes for the length grades are measured from the Y axis while the width grades are measured from the origin point if a common external line is being used. Where a

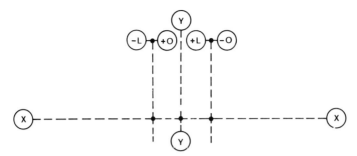

Method 1: where L is equal to O

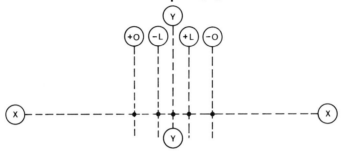

Method 2: where L is less than O

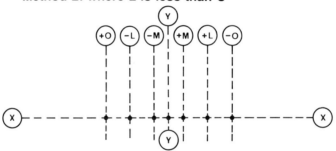

Method 3: incorporating increment M

Fig. 7.4. The axes of length.

grade is based on a common internal line, the width increments are measured from selected external points.

Fig. 7.8 illustrates the marking of individual width increments on the Y axis, and the principle is:

- The value of increment F is measured from the origin point.
- The value of increment G is measured from F.
- The value of increment E is measured from G.

F + G is equal to the across back grade of D and D + E is the total back width grade.

The same markings are repeated on the opposite side of the origin point for the reverse, up or down grade.

The combination of the length and width grade

increments is referred to as the increment net (Fig. 7.9), and this is illustrated in all the example grades.

The preparation stage can be summed up as:

(1) Mark the X and Y axes on the component to be graded.
(2) Copy the base size pattern on to the paper and transfer the X and Y axes.
(3) Establish the origin point of the grade.
(4) Select or calculate the increment values which are appropriate to the size interval being graded.
(5) Mark the length grade secondary axes parallel to the Y axis. Notate them, especially if they are to serve as dual purpose axes.
(6) Mark the width grade increments from the origin

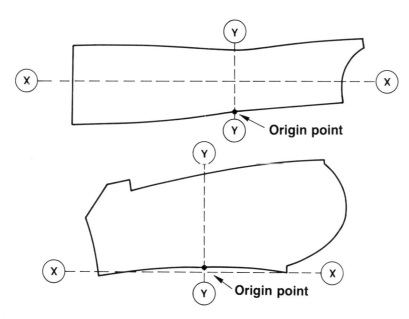

Fig. 7.5. Examples of origin points.

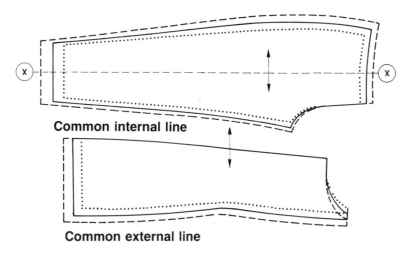

Fig. 7.6. Examples of common origin lines.

point ensuring that they are parallel to the X axis and that the lines intersect the length axes where they are to be used for a width grade on that particular axis.

So much for the preparation, and now for the grading itself.

Grading

The marking should be done with a sharp 1H or 2H pencil or a fine pen. For the novice pattern grader, it would be advisable to use different coloured pens or pencils for each size.

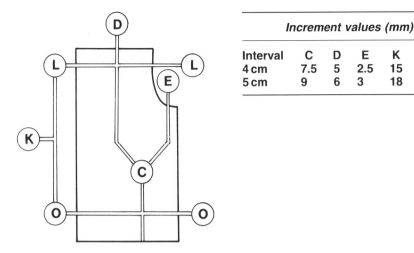

Increment values (mm)						
Interval	C	D	E	K	L	O
4 cm	7.5	5	2.5	15	5	10
5 cm	9	6	3	18	6	12

Fig. 7.7. Grading increments and values.

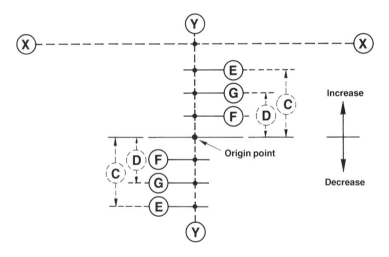

Fig. 7.8. Width increments in relation to origin point.

As some of the grading increments are very small, it is easier to measure when they are used in multiples of more than one size. In practice this means that instead of grading each individual size, only the largest and smallest sizes required are graded from the base pattern. The external and relevant internal points of this 'two-size' grade are then connected by means of a line called a vector, which is not only used for deriving the intermediate sizes but also for checking the accuracy of the grading.

The distance along the vector is measured and then divided by the number of sizes between the base size and graded size *plus one*. For example, if the base size is 36 and the largest size is 44, there are three sizes between them: 38, 40 and 42. Consequently the length

of each vector between size 36 and size 44 would be divided by 4, i.e. three sizes plus one.

Fig. 7.10 illustrates an example of the use of vectors. The points of each intermediate size are joined by using the original pattern, and the completed drawing is called a nested grade.

The next stage is to transfer each size to a separate sheet of paper, using an awl for the straight lines, pocket and dart positions etc., and a needle type tracing wheel for the curved lines. With some experience only the vector points need to be transferred and the individual patterns can be completed with the base size pattern.

This stage of the grading process requires a lot of marking, tracing, cutting and notching and it can be

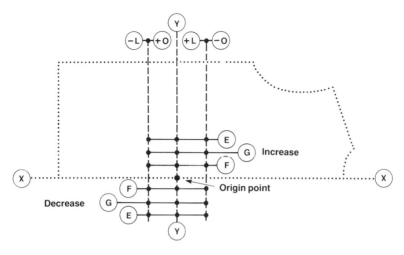

Fig. 7.9. Example of increment net.

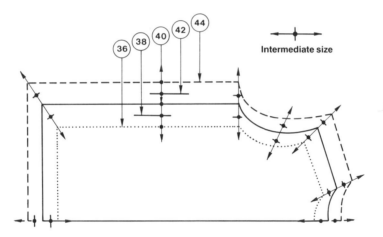

Fig. 7.10. The vector method of grading.

performed efficiently by observing the following guidelines:

- Mark everything possible while holding the pen or pencil.
- Trace everything possible while holding the awl or tracing wheel.
- Cut everything possible while holding the scissors.
- Notch everything possible while holding the notchers.

This way of working eliminates a lot of unnecessary handling involved in continually picking up and putting down different tools.

W&F LTD	
Style No.	*4765*
Garment	*SB JKT*
Size	*42S*
Component	*Front*
Material	*Lining*
Total pieces	*8*

Fig. 7.11. Example of pattern stamp.

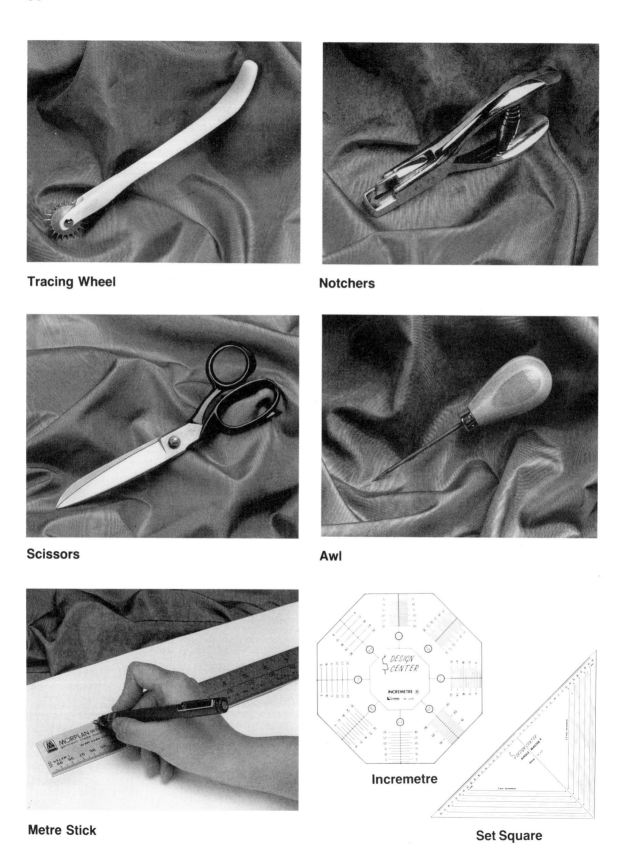

Tracing Wheel

Notchers

Scissors

Awl

Metre Stick

Incremetre

Set Square

Fig. 7.12. Grading tools.

Checking

While the vectors have a control function for individual components, it is always advisable to cross check the grades between constructionally related components. For example, the length grades between the forepart, sidebody and back and those of the top and under sleeves. This cross checking routine should be performed on both top cloth and lining components.

Completion

This, the final stage, is concerned with preparing the patterns for issue to the cutting room. There is one cardinal principle involved: there should be no necessity for the cutting room staff to request information regarding the graded patterns.

In practical terms, this means that style numbers, sizes, grain lines, pocket and dart positions should be clearly marked, together with the type of material for which the pattern is to be used, e.g., cloth, lining, fusible and pocket linings etc. It also helps to give the total number of pattern pieces to be used for cutting a particular material. A useful aid to the systematic presentation of information is a large rubber stamp with sufficient space to include all the necessary details. An example of this type of stamp is shown in Fig. 7.11.

Lastly, a few words regarding tools. As a rule, it is always better to invest in quality tools rather than cheap substitutes. While the original outlay might be considerable, it will prove to be cheaper in the long run to buy the best.

Fig. 7.12 shows the basic tools for grading:

- Metre stick – for all long lines, especially axes.
- Set square – this should have a hypotenuse of at least 40 cm. Used for establishing right angles for axes and drawing short straight lines.
- Incremeter – the grader's best friend. This instrument completely eliminates the necessity for measuring grading increments.
- Awl – used for 'picking-off' individual patterns from the nested grade.
- Tracing wheel – for transferring curved line sections.
- Scissors – for the average person these should be about 24 cm long and should be used only for cutting paper.
- Notchers – there should be a substantial right-angled shoulder behind the blade, which ensures that notches are at the correct angle to the pattern line.

Obviously there are other tools which can be added to this selection, but those illustrated would be sufficient for starting off.

TO SUM UP

Manual grading is a very labour intensive operation but it can be performed at a high level of efficiency if sufficient thought is given to the methods of working. Thorough and accurate preparation is the key.

Chapter 8

The Master Grades

The following demonstration grades are for the basic block patterns of men's wear and they serve as the foundation for grading all the styled garments developed from these blocks.

The grades themselves are broken down into stages, each of which is illustrated and has easy to follow instructions. The pattern section to be marked at each stage is denoted by a thickened line. To become familiar with the techniques involved, it is suggested that each master grade be repeated two or three times so as to establish a practical understanding of the principles involved and an efficient working routine. Once the basic procedures have been mastered, the transfer to more complex grades will be considerably easier.

There is a great deal of expertise involved in pattern grading and this can only be developed through experience and understanding.

8.1 MASTER BODY GRADE

(A) Open necked front

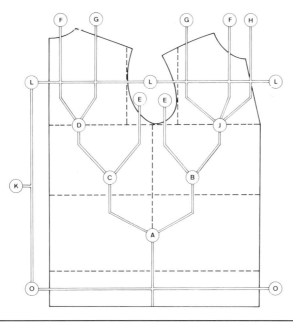

Interval	A	B	C	D	E	F	G	H	J	K	L	O
4 cm	20	12.5	7.5	5	2.5	2.5	2.5	5	10	10	5	5
5 cm	25	16	9	6	3	3	3	7	13	12	6	6

Increment values

Fig. 8.1.1. Master body grade – open necked front.

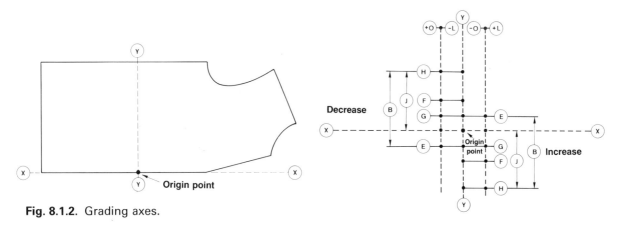

Fig. 8.1.2. Grading axes.

Fig. 8.1.3. Increment net.

Stage 1: Align X and Y axes of pattern and paper
(Fig. 8.1.4).
● Mark central section of armhole.

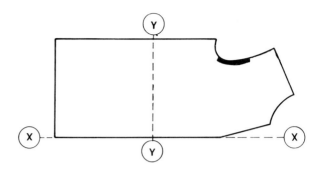

Fig. 8.1.4.

Stage 2: Align Y axes of pattern and paper
(Fig. 8.1.5).
● Align front edge to E.
● Mark corner of armhole and side seam.

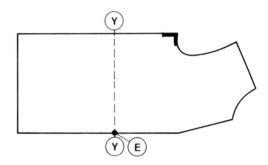

Fig. 8.1.5.

Stage 3: Remain aligned to E (Fig. 8.1.6).
● Align Y axis of pattern to O axis on paper.
● Mark corner of hem and side seam.

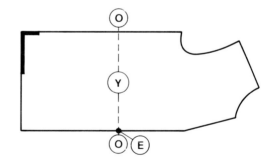

Fig. 8.1.6.

Stage 4: Align front edge to X axis (Fig. 8.1.7).
● Align Y axis of pattern to L axis on paper.
● Mark top part of armhole and start of shoulder.

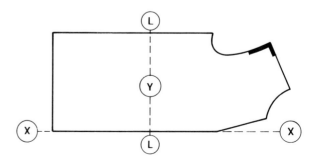

Fig. 8.1.7.

Stage 5:   Remain on L axis (Fig. 8.1.8).
- Align front edge to G.
- Mark front neck point and start of neck line.

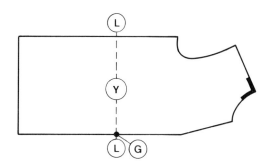

Fig. 8.1.8.

Stage 6:   Remain on L axis (Fig. 8.1.9).
- Align front edge to F.
- Complete neck line.
- Mark start of front edge.

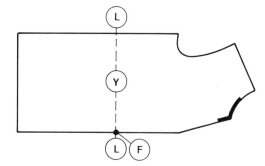

Fig. 8.1.9.

Stage 7:   Align Y axes of pattern and paper (Fig. 8.1.10).
- Move to H.
- Mark front edge from chest line point down.

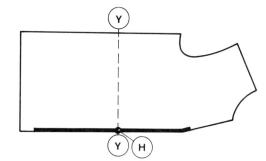

Fig. 8.1.10.

Stage 8:   Remain aligned to H (Fig. 8.1.11).
- Align Y axis of pattern to O axis on paper.
- Complete front edge.
- Complete hem.

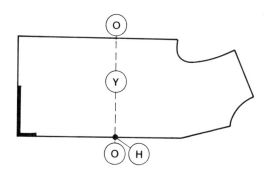

Fig. 8.1.11.

Stage 9:   Use pattern to complete (Fig. 8.1.12):
- Side seam.
- Armhole and shoulder.
- Upper section of front edge.

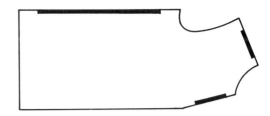

Fig. 8.1.12.

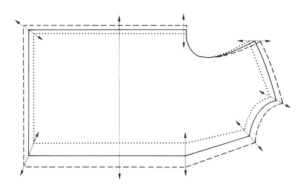

Fig. 8.1.13. Grade for open necked front.

(B)   Back

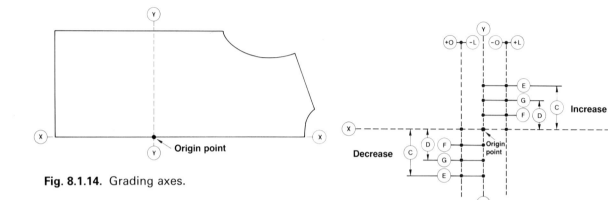

Fig. 8.1.14. Grading axes.

Fig. 8.1.15. Increment net.

Stage 1:   Align Y axes of pattern and paper (Fig. 8.1.16).
- Move CB to D.
- Mark part of armhole from across back line down.

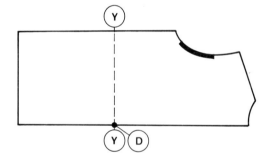

Fig. 8.1.16.

Stage 2:   Remain on Y axis (Fig. 8.1.17).
- Move CB to E.
- Mark corner of armhole and side seam.

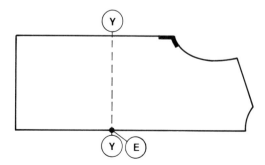

Fig. 8.1.17.

Stage 3:   Remain aligned to E (Fig. 8.1.18).
● Align Y axis of pattern to O axis on paper.
● Mark corner of hem and side seam.

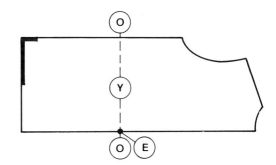

Fig. 8.1.18.

Stage 4:   Remain on O axis (Fig. 8.1.19).
● Align CB to X axis.
● Mark lower section of CB and complete hem.

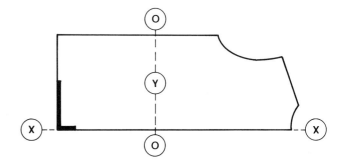

Fig. 8.1.19.

Stage 5:   Remain on X axis (Fig. 8.1.20).
● Align Y axis of pattern to L axis on paper.
● Complete upper section of CB and mark start of neck.

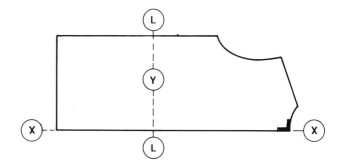

Fig. 8.1.20.

Stage 6:   Remain on L axis (Fig. 8.1.21).
● Align CB to F.
● Complete neck line.
● Mark start of shoulder.

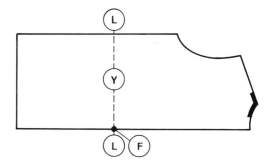

Fig. 8.1.21.

Stage 7: Remain on L axis (Fig. 8.1.22).
- Align CB to G.
- Mark shoulder end and complete armhole.

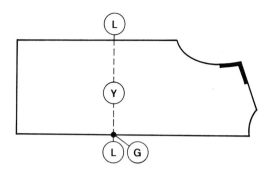

Fig. 8.1.22.

Stage 8: Use pattern to complete (Fig. 8.1.23):
- Side seam.
- Armhole and shoulder.

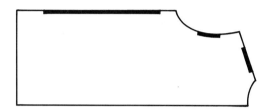

Fig. 8.1.23.

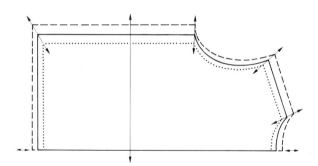

Fig. 8.1.24. Grade for back.

8.2   MASTER BODY GRADE
Closed neck front

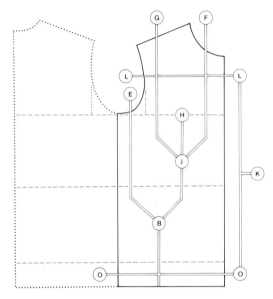

Increment values								
Interval	B	E	F	G	H	J	K	L	O
4 cm	12.5	2.5	2.5	2.5	5	10	10	5	5
5 cm	16	3	3	3	7	13	12	6	6

Back as master grade 4.1

Fig. 8.2.1. Master grade for closed neck front.

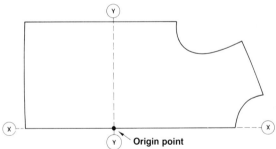

Fig. 8.2.2. Grading axes.

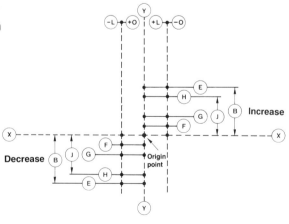

Fig. 8.2.3. Increment net.

Stage 1: Align X and Y axes of pattern and paper (Fig. 8.2.4).
● Mark part of front edge.

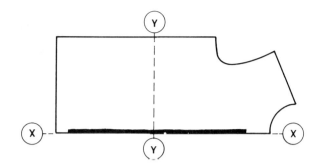

Fig. 8.2.4.

Stage 2: Align Y axes of pattern and paper (Fig. 8.2.5).
● Align front edge to H.
● Mark lower part of armhole.

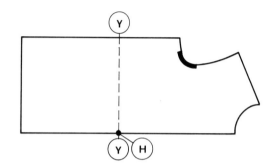

Fig. 8.2.5.

Stage 3: Remain on Y axis (Fig. 8.2.6).
● Move to E.
● Complete lower armhole.
● Mark start of side seam.

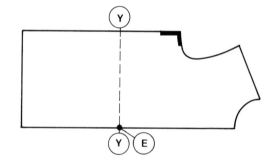

Fig. 8.2.6.

Stage 4: Remain aligned to E (Fig. 8.2.7).
● Align Y axis of pattern to O axis on paper.
● Mark end of side seam.
● Mark part of hem.

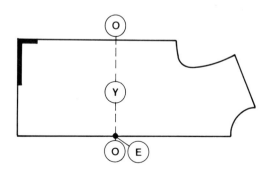

Fig. 8.2.7.

Stage 5: Remain on O axis (Fig. 8.2.8).
- Align front edge to X axis.
- Mark lower section of front edge.
- Complete hem.

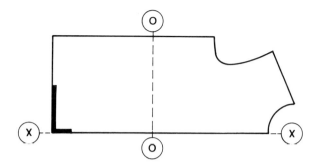

Fig. 8.2.8.

Stage 6: Remain on X axis (Fig. 8.2.9).
- Align Y axis of pattern to L axis on paper.
- Mark corner of CF and neckline.

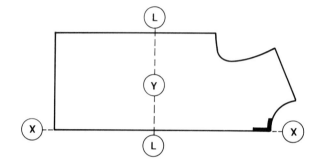

Fig. 8.2.9.

Stage 7: Remain on L axis (Fig. 8.2.10).
- Move to F.
- Complete neck line.
- Mark start of shoulder.

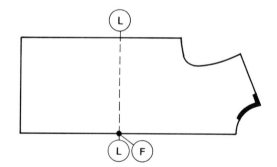

Fig. 8.2.10.

Stage 8: Remain on L axis (Fig. 8.2.11).
- Move to G.
- Mark end of shoulder and start of armhole.

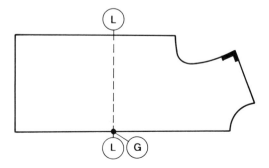

Fig. 8.2.11.

Stage 9: Use pattern to complete (Fig. 8.2.12):
● Side seam and shoulder.

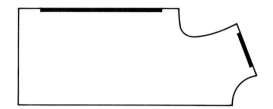

Fig. 8.2.12.

Stage 10: Align shoulder lines of back and front (Fig. 8.2.13).
● Blend armhole run across shoulder line.

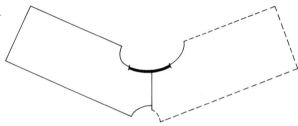

Fig. 8.2.13.

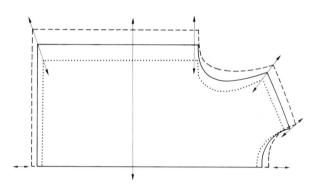

Fig. 8.2.14. Grade for closed neck front.

8.3 MASTER BODY GRADE

(A) Open neck facing

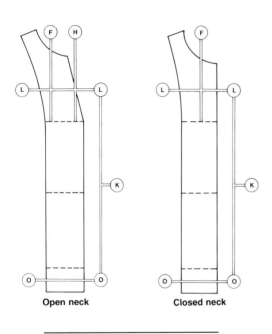

Open neck   Closed neck

Increment values

Interval	F	H	K	L	O
4 cm	2.5	5	10	5	5
5 cm	3	7	12	6	6

Fig. 8.3.1. Master facing grades.

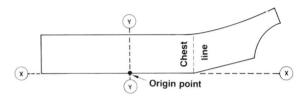

Fig. 8.3.2. Grading axes.

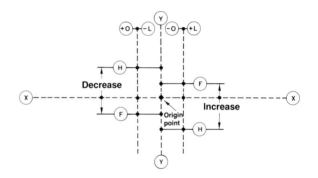

Fig. 8.3.3. Increment net.

Stage 1: Align Y axes of pattern and paper (Fig. 8.3.4).
- Align CF to H.
- Mark CF and inside edge from chest line down.

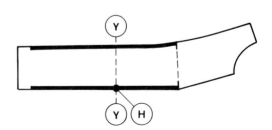

Fig. 8.3.4.

Stage 2:   Remain aligned to H (Fig. 8.3.5).
- Align Y axis of pattern to O axis on paper.
- Complete lower section of facing.

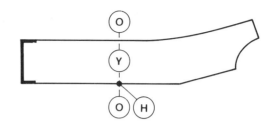

Fig. 8.3.5.

Stage 3:   Align CF to X axis (Fig. 8.3.6).
- Align Y axis of pattern to L axis on paper.
- Mark corner of CF and neck line.

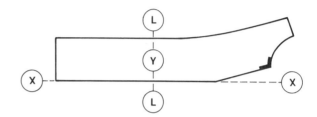

Fig. 8.3.6.

Stage 4:   Remain on L axis (Fig. 8.3.7).
- Move to F.
- Complete neck line.
- Mark shoulder section of facing.

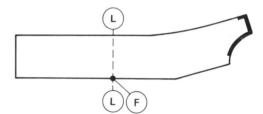

Fig. 8.3.7.

Stage 5:   Use pattern to (Fig. 8.3.8):
- Complete CF.
- Connect shoulder section to inside edge.

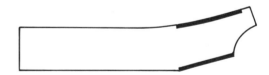

Fig. 8.3.8.

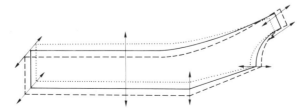

Fig. 8.3.9. Grade for open neck facing.

(B)   Closed neck facing

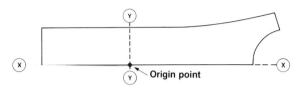

Fig. 8.3.10. Grading axes.

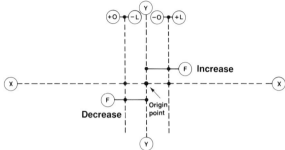

Fig. 8.3.11. Increment net.

Stage 1:   Align X and Y axes of pattern and paper (Fig. 8.3.12).
- Mark part of front edge.
- Mark part of inside edge.

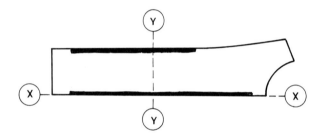

Fig. 8.3.12.

Stage 2:   Align pattern to X axis (Fig. 8.3.13).
- Align Y axis of pattern to O axis on paper.
- Mark lower end of facing.

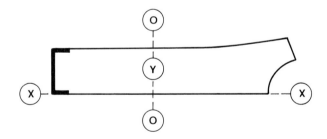

Fig. 8.3.13.

Stage 3:   Remain on Y axis (Fig. 8.3.14).
- Align Y axis of pattern to L axis on paper.
- Mark corner of CF and neck line.

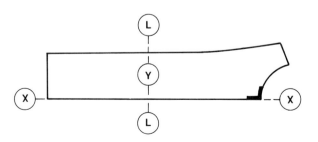

Fig. 8.3.14.

Stage 4:   Remain on L axis (Fig. 8.3.15).
● Move to F.
● Complete neck line.
● Mark shoulder section of facing.

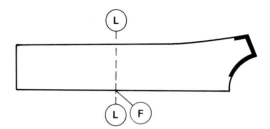

Fig. 8.3.15.

Stage 5:   Use pattern to (Fig. 8.3.16):
join shoulder section to inside edge at chest line.

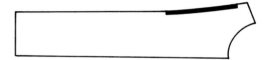

Fig. 8.3.16.

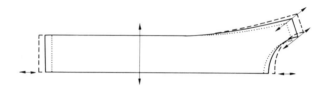

Fig. 8.3.17.   Grade for closed neck facing.

8.4   MASTER GRADE
One piece sleeve

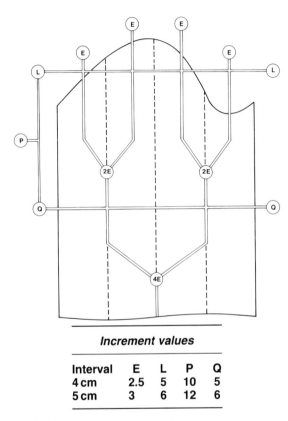

Increment values				
Interval	E	L	P	Q
4 cm	2.5	5	10	5
5 cm	3	6	12	6

Fig. 8.4.1. Master sleeve grade.

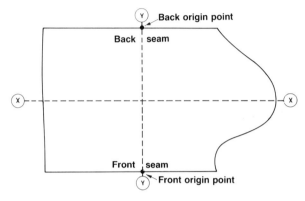

Fig. 8.4.2. Grading axes.

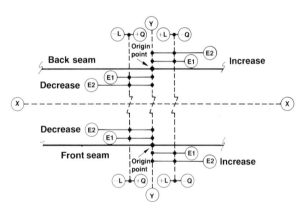

Fig. 8.4.3. Increment net.

Stage 1:   Align X axes of pattern and paper (Fig. 8.4.4).
- Align Y axis of pattern to L axis on paper.
- Mark vertex of crown.

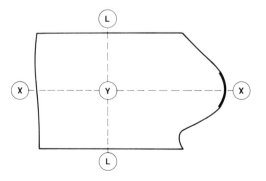

Fig. 8.4.4.

Stage 2: Remain on Y axis (Fig. 8.4.5).
● Align Y axis of pattern to Q axis on paper.
● Mark centre section of cuff.

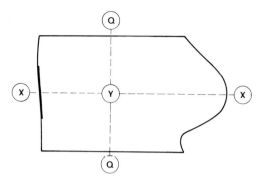

Fig. 8.4.5.

BACK WIDTH GRADE

Stage 3: Align Y axes of pattern and paper (Fig. 8.4.6).
● Align back seam to E1.
● Mark section of back sleeve head.

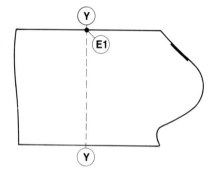

Fig. 8.4.6.

Stage 4: Remain on Y axis (Fig. 8.4.7).
● Align back seam to E2.
● Mark lower section of head and start of underarm seam.

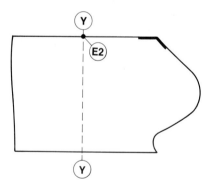

Fig. 8.4.7.

Stage 5: Remain aligned to E2 (Fig. 8.4.8).
- Align Y axis of pattern to Q axis on paper.
- Mark end of underseam and complete the back cuff.

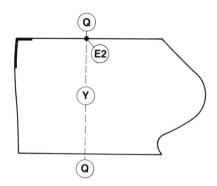

Fig. 8.4.8.

FRONT WIDTH GRADE

Stage 6: Remain aligned to Q axis (Fig. 8.4.9).
- Align front seam to E2.
- Complete the front cuff and mark end of underseam.

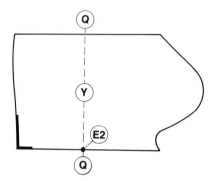

Fig. 8.4.9.

Stage 7: Remain aligned to E2 (Fig. 8.4.10).
- Align Y axes of pattern and paper.
- Mark top of underseam and part of undersleeve.

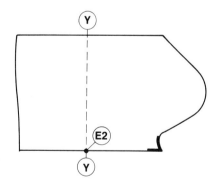

Fig. 8.4.10.

Stage 8:   Remain on Y axis (Fig. 8.4.11).
- Align underseam to E1.
- Mark section of front sleeve head.

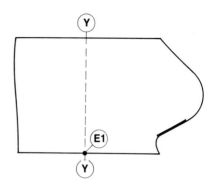

Fig. 8.4.11.

Stage 9:   Use pattern to (Fig. 8.4.12):
- Complete back and front underseams.
- Blend sleeve head.

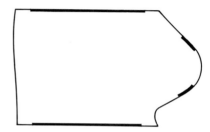

Fig. 8.4.12.

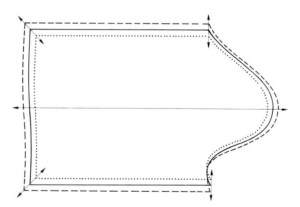

Fig. 8.4.13.   Grade for one-piece sleeve.

8.5   MASTER GRADE
Basic trouser

The following demonstration grading is an example of a dynamic length grade. Some other features of this grade are:

- The working method is based on a centre line which runs down the length of the panel and the width grades are performed on either side, towards or away from this line. As a result, three width grade axes lines are used.

- The values given for the thigh, knee and bottom increments can be increased or decreased. From the size charts analysed, there is very little uniformity in the amounts by which these three girths are graded.

Finally, the pattern for a trouser leg is long and unwieldly and during grading care should be taken to ensure the accurate marking and alignment of the axes.

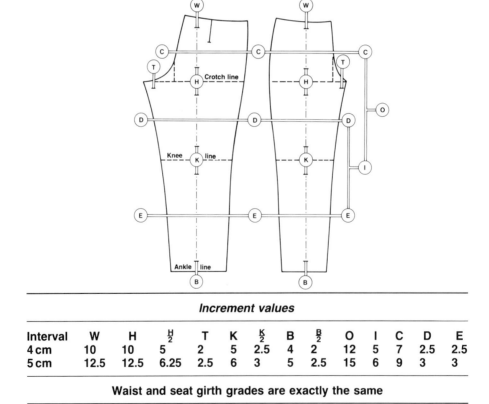

Increment values

Interval	W	H	$\frac{H}{2}$	T	K	$\frac{K}{2}$	B	$\frac{B}{2}$	O	I	C	D	E
4 cm	10	10	5	2	5	2.5	4	2	12	5	7	2.5	2.5
5 cm	12.5	12.5	6.25	2.5	6	3	5	2.5	15	6	9	3	3

Waist and seat girth grades are exactly the same

Fig. 8.5.1. Grading increments for basic trouser.

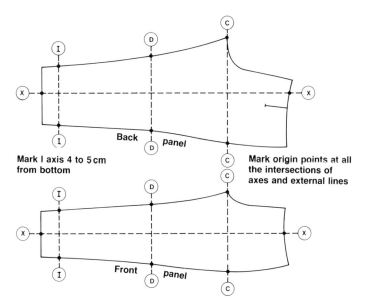

Fig. 8.5.2. Grading axes for back and front trouser panels.

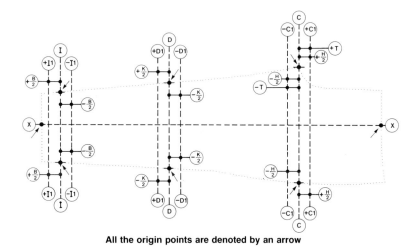

All the origin points are denoted by an arrow

Fig. 8.5.3. Increment net for back and front trouser panels.

(A)   Top side (front)

Stage 1:   Align C axes of pattern and paper (Fig. 8.5.4).

- Align side seam origin point to $\frac{H}{2}$.
- Mark hip area of side seam.

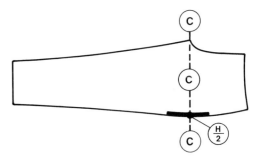

Fig. 8.5.4.

Stage 2:   Remain aligned on C axis (Fig. 8.5.5).

- Align crotch point to $\frac{H}{2}$.
- Mark lower section of fly seam.

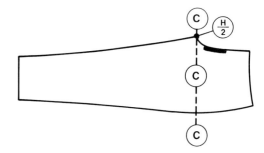

Fig. 8.5.5.

Stage 3:   Remain aligned to C axis (Fig. 8.5.6).
- Align crotch point to T.
- Complete lower section of fly seam.
- Mark start of inside leg seam.

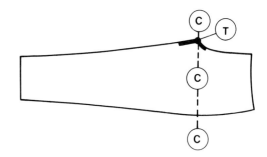

Fig. 8.5.6.

Stage 4:   Align C axis of pattern to C1 axis on paper (Fig. 8.5.7).

- Align origin point to $\frac{H}{2}$ at side seam.
- Mark rest of side seam to waist line.
- Mark part of waist line.

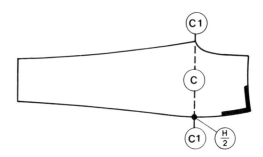

Fig. 8.5.7.

Stage 5: Remain aligned to C1 axis (Fig. 8.5.8).

- Align crotch point to $\dfrac{H}{2}$.
- Complete fly seam.
- Complete waist line.

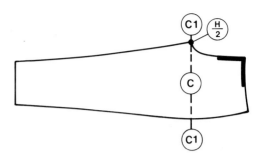

Fig. 8.5.8.

Stage 6: Align D axis of pattern to D1 axis on paper (Fig. 8.5.9).

- Align origin point on inside leg seam to $\dfrac{K}{2}$.
- Mark central section of inside leg.

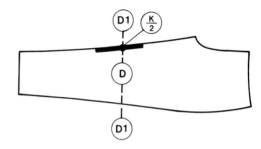

Fig. 8.5.9.

Stage 7: Remain aligned to D1 axis (Fig. 8.5.10).

- Align origin point on side seam to $\dfrac{K}{2}$.
- Mark central section of side seam.

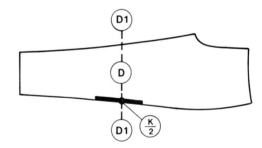

Fig. 8.5.10.

Stage 8: Align I axis of pattern to I1 axis on paper (Fig. 8.5.11).

- Align origin point on inside leg seam to $\dfrac{B}{2}$.
- Complete inside leg seam.
- Mark part of bottom.

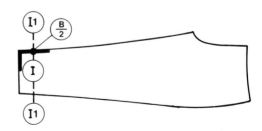

Fig. 8.5.11.

64

Stage 9:   Remain aligned on I1 axis (Fig. 8.5.12).

- Align origin point on side seam to $\frac{B}{2}$.

- Complete side seam.
- Complete bottom.

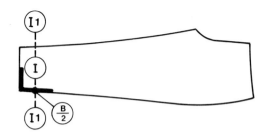

Fig. 8.5.12.

Stage 10:   Use pattern to (Fig. 8.5.13):
- Blend inside leg seam.
- Blend side seam.

Fig. 8.5.13.

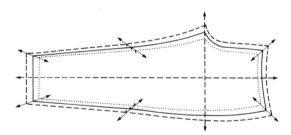

Fig. 8.5.14. Grade for front trouser panel.

(B) Underside (back)

Stage 1:   Align C axes of pattern and paper
(Fig. 8.5.15).

- Align side seam origin point to $\frac{H}{2}$.

- Mark hip area of side seam.

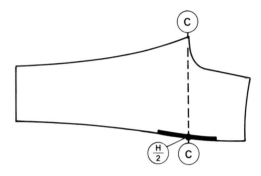

Fig. 8.5.15.

Stage 2:   Remain aligned on C axis (Fig. 8.5.16).

- Align crotch point to $\frac{H}{2}$.

- Mark part of lower section of seat seam.

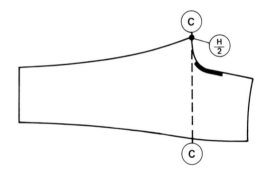

Fig. 8.5.16.

Stage 3:   Remain aligned on C axis (Fig. 8.5.17).
- Align crotch point to T.
- Complete lower section of seat seam.
- Mark start of inside leg seam.

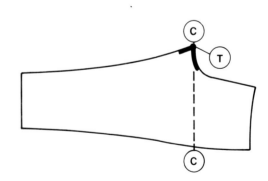

Fig. 8.5.17.

Stage 4: Align X axes of pattern and paper
(Fig. 8.5.18).
- Align C axis of pattern to C1 axis on paper.
- Mark dart and two or three centimetres on either
  side along waist line.

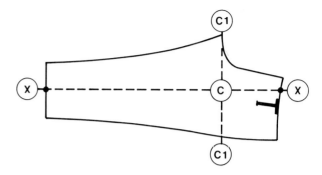

Fig. 8.5.18.

Stage 5: Remain aligned to C1 axis (Fig. 8.5.19).
- Align origin point to $\frac{H}{2}$ at side seam.
- Mark rest of side seam to waist line.
- Mark waist line to dart.

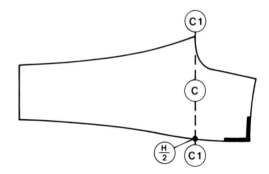

Fig. 8.5.19.

Stage 6: Remain aligned to C1 axis (Fig. 8.5.20).
- Align crotch point to $\frac{H}{2}$.
- Complete seat seam.
- Complete waist line.

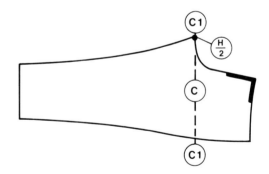

Fig. 8.5.20.

Stage 7:   Align D axis of pattern to D1 axis on paper (Fig. 8.5.21).

- Align origin point on inside leg seam to $\dfrac{K}{2}$.

- Mark central section of inside leg.

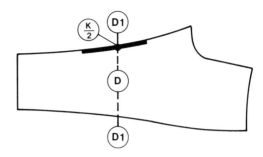

Fig. 8.5.21.

Stage 8:   Remain aligned on D1 axis (Fig. 8.5.22).

- Align origin point on side seam to $\dfrac{K}{2}$.

- Mark central section of side seam.

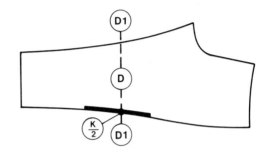

Fig. 8.5.22.

Stage 9:   Align I axis of pattern to I1 axis on paper (Fig. 8.5.23).

- Align origin point on inside leg seam to $\dfrac{B}{2}$.

- Complete inside leg seam.
- Mark part of bottom.

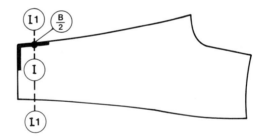

Fig. 8.5.23.

Stage 10:   Remain aligned to I1 axis (Fig. 8.5.24).

- Align origin point on side seam to $\dfrac{B}{2}$.

- Complete side seam.
- Complete bottom.

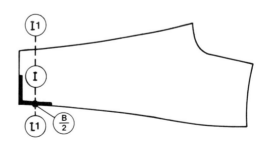

Fig. 8.5.24.

Stage 11: Use pattern to (Fig. 8.5.25):
- Blend inside leg seam.
- Blend side seam.

Fig. 8.5.25.

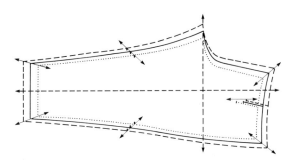

Fig. 8.5.26. Grade for back trouser panel.

Chapter 9

Industrial Pattern Grading

The question of proportions

The objective of pattern grading is not just to produce patterns in different sizes but also to maintain the original design proportions of the style being graded. However, to achieve these two objectives in the optimum fashion is not always possible because of the standardisation of many manufacturing operations. As a result, pattern grading should always be accurate as regards sizing but it must also include some very practical concessions to the process technology used for some of the design features of garments.

To apply these concessions with an understanding of their effects, the first stage would be to examine the proportional aspects of pattern grading. The most appropriate example for this is the joined forepart and sidebody of a man's jacket because this assembly contains within it a view of the collar and lapel, a pocket and an outbreast welt. Fig. 9.1 shows a front with these components where the flapped patch can be taken for example purposes as representing a patch, flapped or jetted jacket. Superimposed are the increments which would be used to grade the forepart and sidebody.

When this assembly is graded up or down changes occur in its length and width and this modifies the dimensional framework within which the collar, lapel and pockets are located. Therefore it follows that if the sizes of these features were left unchanged, their relative proportions to the overall size of the front would alter from size to size, as follows.

THE COLLAR AND LAPEL

This section of the garment is one of the major fashion features in menswear, with most of the changes being made in the collar length and lapel width. These two factors are set against a framework which has very definite boundaries, with the collar and lapel proportions being relative to these boundaries. Fig. 9.2A illustrates the length and width framework and the positions of the main dimensions for the collar and lapel, and Fig. 9.2B shows the grading increments that are applied to this area of the garment.

Lapel width for a particular style is very often

included in the sizing specification issued by retailers, and with very rare exceptions it remains static for all the sizes in the range. This, coupled with a two or three size collar length system has the following effect when this area is graded in the width by increment J and in the length by increment L:

Larger sizes   The lapel becomes proportionately narrower and longer as the sizes increase.
Smaller sizes   The lapel becomes proportionately wider and shorter as the sizes decrease.

Thus in both cases the design proportions in relation to the base size are affected, very noticeably so at the top and bottom of the size range.

There is no universal method of collar and lapel grading because of the varying requirements of retailers and/or the technological limitations of the factory. Nevertheless there are some alternative methods which are used according to the circumstances and two of these are demonstrated in Part 4.

POCKETS

These are not always a prominent design feature but they nevertheless have an influence on design balance. Some prime examples of how grading can affect this balance are given here.

FLAPPED POCKETS

The original pattern for a flap is constructed with a definite relationship between its length and width, its length being proportionate to the width of the front at the line of the pocket height (Fig. 9.3A). As this width changes from size to size by the applications of increments 2E and J (Fig. 9.3B), it would seem reasonable to grade the length of the flap in proportion to this change. So logically, if the flap length changes so should its width in order to maintain the original proportions.

There is no simple answer because as with collars and lapels, the extent to which flaps can be graded is governed in the main, by technological factors.

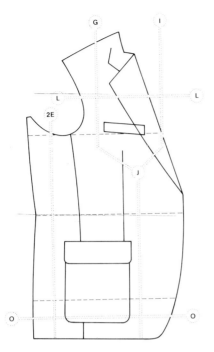

Fig. 9.1. Example jacket front.

PATCH POCKETS

A patch pocket is located in a framework in length from the waist line to the hem, and in width from the front edge to the side seam (Fig. 9.4A). The length and width of this area is changed by the applications of increment J, 2E and O (Fig. 9.4B). There is therefore more than just a theoretical justification for the grading of patch pockets which are applied to the front by semi or fully automatic systems.

OUTBREAST WELT POCKETS

This type of pocket is conventionally positioned slantwise on the chest line and its length is a proportion of the across chest width (Fig. 9.5A). As this width changes from size to size by the application of increment J, (Fig. 9.5B) it would seem correct to change the welt length and position accordingly, especially if the lapel width is static for all or part of the size range.

VENTS

While the length of vents is not usually influenced by technological or other factors, vents are part of the

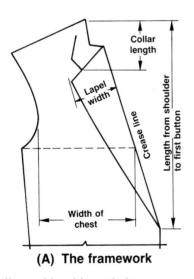

(A) The framework

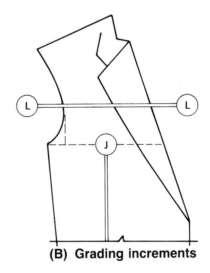

(B) Grading increments

Fig. 9.2. Collar and lapel boundaries.

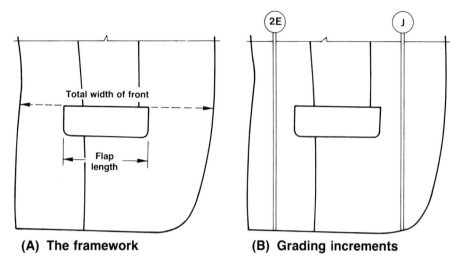

(A) The framework **(B) Grading increments**

Fig. 9.3. Flap boundaries.

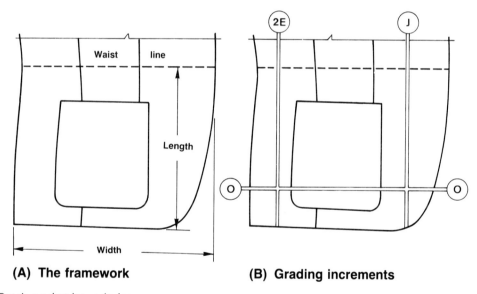

(A) The framework **(B) Grading increments**

Fig. 9.4. Patch pocket boundaries.

design balance and should be graded accordingly. Fig. 9.6A illustrates the length relationships between the garment and vent lengths whilst Fig. 9.6B shows the increments used for the length grades. An example of how these length proportions are maintained during grading is demonstrated in Chapter 6.

TO SUM UP

This chapter has attempted to demonstrate in practical terms the necessity for an adaptable system for the detailed grading of menswear. Technology, customers' requirements and garment design generate many different situations and effective grading is really the sum total of all aspects, large and small.

Garment technology and pattern grading

The staple items of men's clothing have a very conventional structure and it is this orthodoxy which

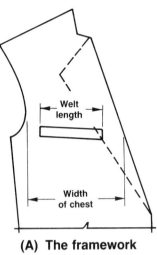

(A) The framework

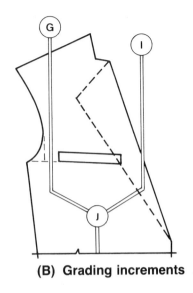

(B) Grading increments

Fig. 9.5. Outbreast welt pocket boundaries.

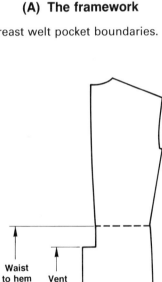

(A) The framework

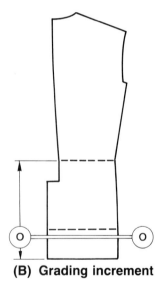

(B) Grading increment

Fig. 9.6. Central back vent boundaries.

enables many of the production processes for menswear to be highly engineered. As a result, the flexibility of many operations is restricted by the limitations of the machinery employed and the investments involved in peripheral equipment. In this context, high-tech leads to standardisation and means acceptable compromises must be made between what should be done and what is viable. The nub of these compromises is the extent of uniformity allowable within the overall framework of cost effectiveness. In other words, the name of the game is money.

This element of standardisation influences some of the more detailed aspects of pattern grading, and the extent of this influence is dictated by the flexibility of the mediums employed. Some examples are given here.

COLLARS

The press-cutting of collars (Fig. 9.7) is a common operation and theoretically each size for a particular style should have its own die. This is a viable

Fig. 9.7. Swing arm hydraulic clicker press.

proposition if large quantities are to be produced in each size. But what if a manufacturer is running a variety of collar styles in small batches only – a situation typical of a product oriented market?

Under these circumstances a practical compromise would be to use one die size for two or even three garment sizes. Collars and necks would then have to be graded accordingly, which in turn affects the grading of lapels.

POCKETS

Pocket flaps for jackets, coats and trousers are components where a standardisation is very often utilised. Most factories use jig sewing machines (Fig. 9.8) for sewing round flaps and these jigs can range from simple plastic forms guided by the operator to sophisticated devices completely machine controlled.

Irrespective of the type of jig used Fig. 9.9, it could be very costly to prepare jigs for each individual size so once again two or three jigs could be considered sufficient to cover all sizes. This is another compromise which influences pattern grading.

The same considerations which apply to pocket flaps are also relevant to the outbreast welt. These pockets are generally pre-creased and folded by a special machine which has a set of dies for folding the welt to a pre-determined length. Different lengths require different dies and it is not unknown for only two

Fig. 9.8. Jig sewing machine.

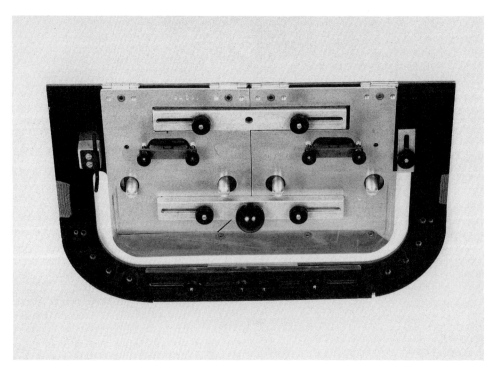

Fig. 9.9. Pocket flap jig.

different welt lengths to be used for all the garment sizes produced by the factory. Pattern grading would also need to take this into account.

Patch pockets are another component which, depending on the finish required, are subject to a degree of standardisation.

Regular bluffed-on pockets (with or without top stitching) do not present any grading compromises because there are no mechanical restrictions on the size of the pocket. However, when patch pockets are prepared and/or attached to foreparts by semi or fully automatic systems, the use of form jigs is central to these operations. As with any other jig-dependent operation, some concessions might be made on the range of jig sizes and this would affect the grading of these components.

Apart from process technology there is another aspect of standardisation which concerns the secondary, or internal, trimmings for garments, i.e., pocket linings and certain fusible interlining components.

For practical purposes internal trimmings can be classified under three headings:

(1) Those specific in form and size for each size of a particular style, for example the front fusible interlining. Obviously this trim would be graded exactly like the top cloth component.
(2) Those specific in form for a group of styles but not necessarily individually sized, for example the chest pieces for double-breasted or single-breasted styles. In this case two sizes for each style group could be used.
(3) Those with a grossed form and used on the

majority of garments irrespective of style and without relating to individual or groups of sizes. Here, one size only would be used.

While it can justifiably be argued that some materials waste is incurred by cutting one or two sizes as against cutting each individual size, there are some practical considerations involved which to a large extent offset this:

- Pattern engineering is simpler and more effective when dealing with a minimum of shapes and sizes.
- Storage and sorting is simplified because of the limited variety.
- The issue of these trimmings to the fusing or sewing departments is not tied down to individual bundles and sizes; they can be issued in bulk to the work station(s) and replenished when necessary. The resultant reduction in sorting and handling is a small but worthwhile saving in labour costs.
- Work stations are simpler to design and operate when they are planned around the positioning of relatively few items.

TO SUM UP

To be truly effective pattern grading has to be something far more than just a rigid technique for producing patterns in different sizes. It not only has to size garments accurately but must also take into account the technology and standardisation systems employed within each factory.

PART 4

APPLICATIONS TO STYLED GARMENTS

Introduction

This part contains examples of the grades for a selection of classic and styled garments, chosen to demonstrate a wide spectrum of grading applications.

The grades themselves are all derived from the master grades in Chapter 8 and they show the explicit relationship between the grade for a block pattern and the grade for a pattern developed from the block. For example, in this part, the grades for eight different types of sleeves are demonstrated and they all have the same root: the master grade for a one piece sleeve.

Making the transfer from the grades for blocks to those for styled patterns requires a small measure of pre-planning in order to allocate increments, wholly or in parts, to the various components of the pattern. The guiding principle is that within the total grade the design feature proportions should be observed as closely as possible. The acid test for really professional grading is that each size of a specific style should be correctly sized and as aesthetically pleasing as the original base size design.

Chapter 10

Single Breasted Jacket with Patch Pocket and Centre Back Vent

The grading features of this demonstration are:

- The lapel width and front collar length remain static for all sizes. This is only one method for grading these components; another variation is shown in Chapter 13.

- Proportional grades are shown for the patch and out breast welt and also for the length of the CB vent.
- The grades for a basic collar and neck piece are also demonstrated.

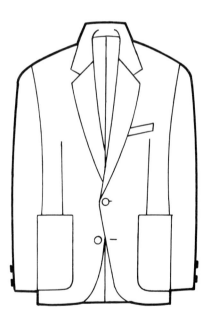 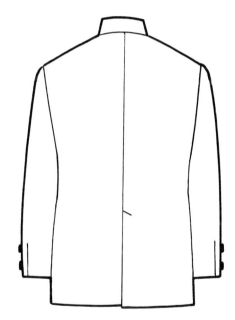

Fig. 10.1. Single breasted jacket.

Grading instructions:
FOREPART

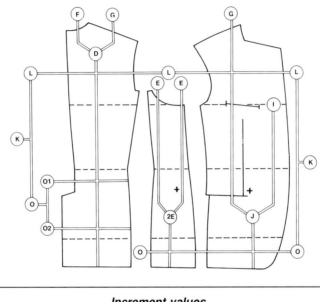

Increment values

Interval	D	E	F	G	I	J	K	L	O	O1	O2
4 cm	5	2.5	2.5	2.5	7.5	10	10	5	5	2	3
5 cm	6	3	3	3	10	13	12	6	6	2	4

Fig. 10.2. Grading increments for body.

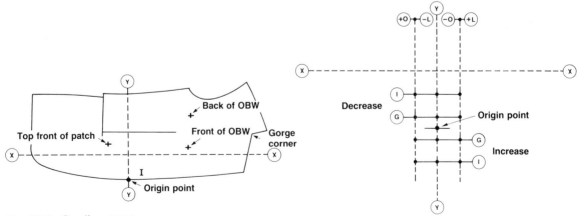

Fig. 10.3. Grading axes.

Fig. 10.4. Increment net.

Stage 1: Align pattern to X and Y axes (Fig. 10.5).
- Mark front side seam and part of armhole.
- Mark start of pocket wedge.
- Mark back end of welt position.

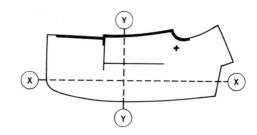

Fig. 10.5.

Stage 2: Remain on Y axis (Fig. 10.6).
- Align front edge to G.
- Mark dart and end of wedge.
- Mark top front of patch pocket.
- Mark front end of welt position.

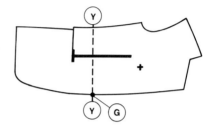

Fig. 10.6.

Stage 3: Remain on Y axis (Fig. 10.7).
- Align front edge to I.
- Mark start of lapel, button stand and start of cutaway line.

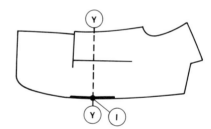

Fig. 10.7.

Stage 4: Remain aligned to I (Fig. 10.8).
- Align Y axis of pattern to O axis on paper.
- Complete cutaway line.
- Mark part of hem.

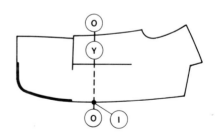

Fig. 10.8.

Stage 5: Remain aligned to O axis (Fig. 10.9).
● Align front edge to origin point.
● Complete front side seam and hem.

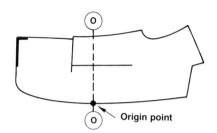

Fig. 10.9.

Stage 6: Align X axes of pattern and paper (Fig. 10.10).
● Align Y axis of pattern to L axis on paper.
● Complete armhole and mark start of shoulder.

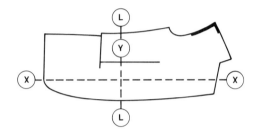

Fig. 10.10.

Stage 7: Remain aligned to L axis (Fig. 10.11).
● Align front edge to G.
● Mark start of shoulder.
● Mark collar seam to gorge corner.

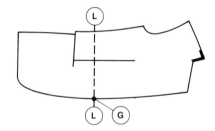

Fig. 10.11.

Stage 8: Pivot pattern from gorge corner until lower lapel edge touches the button stand line marked in stage 3 (Fig. 10.12).
● Mark collar seam and lapel.
● Mark lapel step.

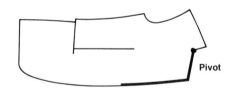

Fig. 10.12.

Stage 9: Use pattern to (Fig. 10.13):
● Complete the shoulder line.
● Blend the lapel and front edge lines.

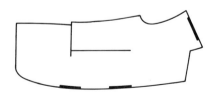

Fig. 10.13.

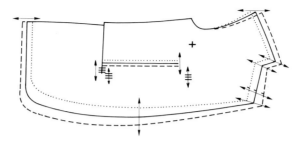

Fig. 10.14. Forepart grade.

Grading instructions:
SIDE BODY

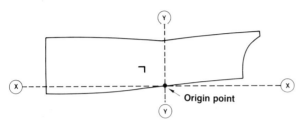

Fig. 10.15. Grading axes

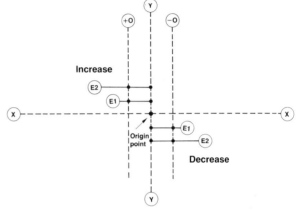

Fig. 10.16. Increment net.

Stage 1: Align X and Y axes of pattern and paper (Fig. 10.17).
- Mark part of front side seam.
- Mark lower section of armhole.

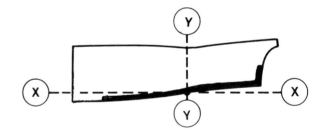

Fig. 10.17.

Stage 2: Align Y axes of pattern and paper (Fig. 10.18).
- Align origin point to E1.
- Mark top corner of patch pocket.

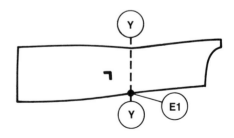

Fig. 10.18.

Stage 3: Remain on Y axis (Fig. 10.19).
- Align origin point to E2.
- Complete lower section of armhole.
- Mark side seam to seat line.

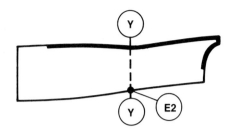

Fig. 10.19.

Stage 4: Remain aligned to E2 (Fig. 10.20).
- Align Y axis of pattern to O axis on paper.
- Complete side seam.
- Mark part of hem.

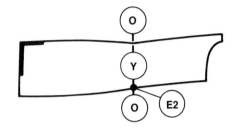

Fig. 10.20.

Stage 5: Remain on O axis (Fig. 10.21).
- Align origin point to intersection of X and O axes.
- Complete front side seam and remainder of hem.

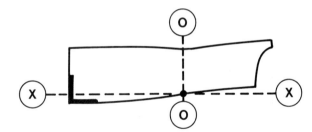

Fig. 10.21.

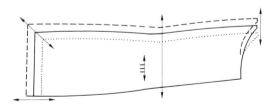

Fig. 10.22. Grade for side body.

Grading instructions:
BACK

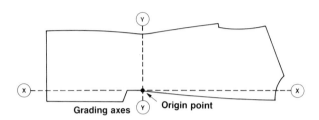

Fig. 10.23. Grading axes.

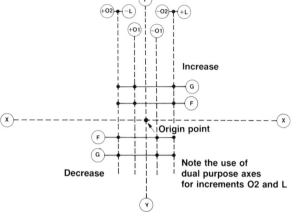

Fig. 10.24. Increment net.

Stage 1: Align X axes of pattern and paper (Fig. 10.25).
- Align Y axis of pattern to O1 axis on paper.
- Mark top section of vent.
- Mark central section of CB.

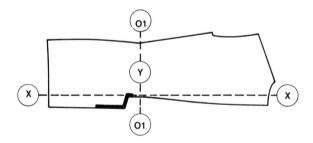

Fig. 10.25.

Stage 2: Remain aligned on X axes (Fig. 10.26).
- Align Y axis of pattern to O2 axis on paper.
- Complete lower section of vent.
- Mark part of hem.

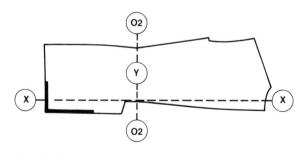

Fig. 10.26.

Stage 3: Remain on O2 axis (Fig. 10.27).
● Align origin point to G.
● Complete hem.
● Mark lower part of side seam.

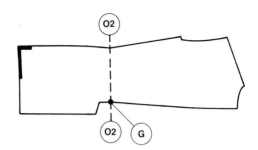

Fig. 10.27.

Stage 4: Align Y axes of pattern and paper (Fig. 10.28).
● Align origin point to G.
● Mark side seam and part of armhole.

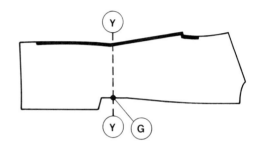

Fig. 10.28.

Stage 5: Align X axis of pattern and paper (Fig. 10.29).
● Align Y axis of pattern to L axis on paper.
● Complete CB seam.
● Mark corner of CB and neckline.

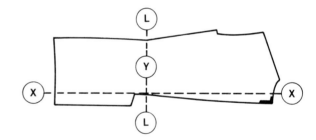

Fig. 10.29.

Stage 6: Remain aligned to L axis (Fig. 10.30).
● Align origin point to F.
● Complete neck line and mark start of shoulder.

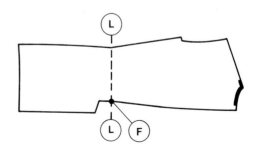

Fig. 10.30.

Stage 7: Remain aligned to L axis (Fig. 10.31).
- Align origin point to G.
- Mark shoulder end and start of armhole.

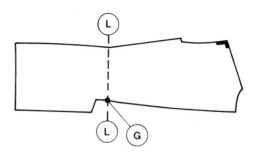

Fig. 10.31.

Stage 8: Use pattern to (Fig. 10.32):
- Complete shoulder.
- Blend armhole.
- Complete CB.

Fig. 10.32.

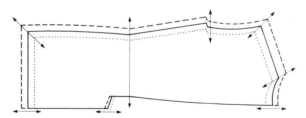

Fig. 10.33. Grade for back.

Grading instructions:
FACING

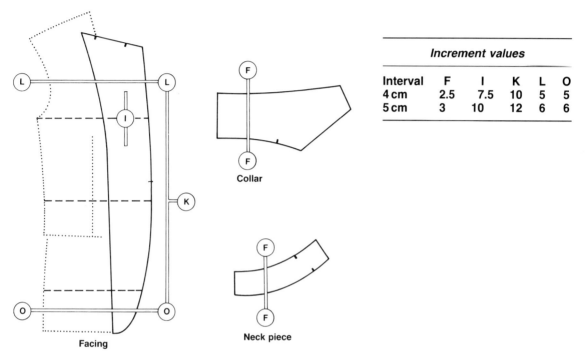

Increment values					
Interval	F	I	K	L	O
4 cm	2.5	7.5	10	5	5
5 cm	3	10	12	6	6

Collar

Facing

Neck piece

Fig. 10.34. Grading increments for facing, collar and neck piece.

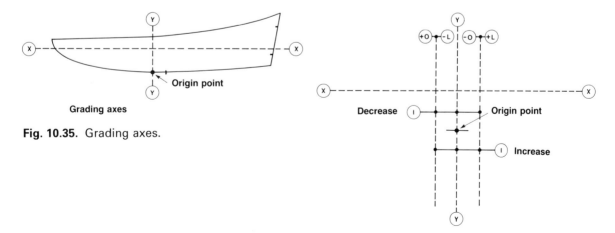

Origin point

Grading axes

Fig. 10.35. Grading axes.

Decrease

Origin point

Increase

Fig. 10.36. Increment net.

Stage 1:   Align Y axes of pattern and paper
(Fig. 10.37).
- Align origin point to I.
- Mark start of lapel, button stand and start of
  cutaway.
- Mark inside edge opposite the marked section of
  the front edge.

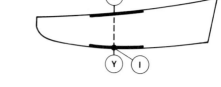

Fig. 10.37.

Stage 2:   Stay aligned to I (Fig. 10.38).
- Align Y axis of pattern to O axis on paper.
- Complete lower section of facing.

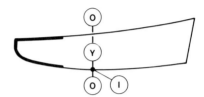

Fig. 10.38.

Stage 3:   Align X axes of pattern and paper
(Fig. 10.39).
- Align Y axis of pattern to L axis on paper.
- Mark corner of inside edge and collar seam.

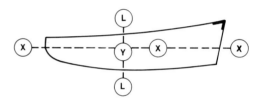

Fig. 10.39.

Stage 4:   Pivot pattern from the corner marked in
Stage 3 until the lapel edge touches the button stand
line (Fig. 10.40).
- Mark collar seam and lapel edge.
- Mark nips on collar seam.

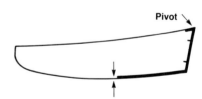

Fig. 10.40.

Stage 5:   Use pattern to complete the inside edge
(Fig. 10.41).

Fig. 10.41.

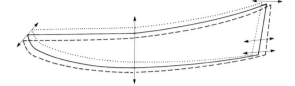

Fig. 10.42. Grade for facing.

In this example, the collar and neck piece are graded by increasing or decreasing the back neck length of the component, i.e. from CB to shoulder nip, by the selected value of increment F.

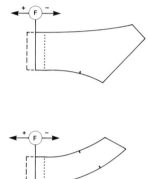

Fig. 10.43. Grades for collar and neck piece.

Grading instructions:
PATCH POCKET AND OUTBREAST WELT

This is an optional grade for the patch pocket which ensures that its proportions, in relation to the forepart, are maintained for each size. Alternatively, the principles of this grade can be applied when, possibly, only two or three different sizes of patches are used for a complete range of sizes.

(A)

This is also an optional proportionate grade for the outbreast welt and can be used in the same situations as those for the patch pocket.

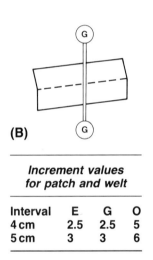

(B)

Increment values
for patch and welt

Interval	E	G	O
4 cm	2.5	2.5	5
5 cm	3	3	6

Fig. 10.44. Increments for patch and outbreast welt.

(A)   Patch pocket

**The X axis of the patch is parallel
to the X axis of the forepart**

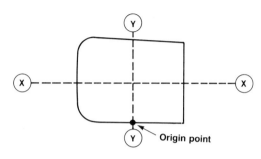

Fig. 10.45. Grading axes.

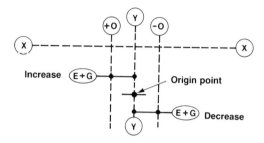

Fig. 10.46. Increment net.

Stage 1: Align X and Y axes of pattern and paper
(Fig. 10.47).
- Mark front of pocket opening.
- Mark part of front edge.

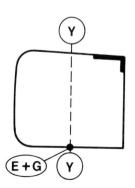

Fig. 10.47.

Stage 2: Remain on Y axis (Fig. 10.48).
- Align origin point to E + G.
- Mark back of pocket opening.
- Mark part of back edge.

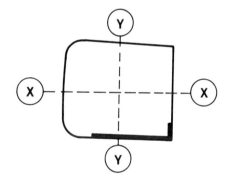

Fig. 10.48.

Stage 3: Align Y axis of pattern to O axis on paper (Fig. 10.49).
- Align origin point to E + G.
- Mark lower part of back edge and part of bottom edge.

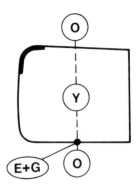

Fig. 10.49.

Stage 4: Remain on O axis (Fig. 10.50).
- Align X axes of pattern and paper.
- Complete front edge.
- Complete bottom edge.

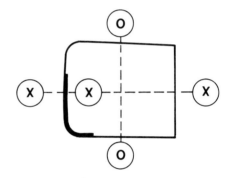

Fig. 10.50.

Stage 5: Use pattern to (Fig. 10.51):
- Complete the back edge.
- Complete the pocket opening.

Fig. 10.51.

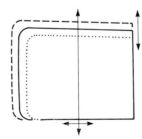

Fig. 10.52. Grade for patch pocket.

(B)   Outbreast welt

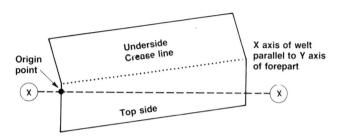

Fig. 10.53. Grading axes.

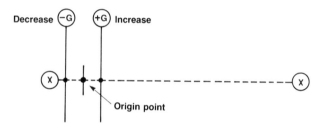

Fig. 10.54. Increment net.

Stage 1:   Align X axes of pattern and paper (Fig. 10.55).
- Mark front edge and start of seam.
- Mark start of crease line.

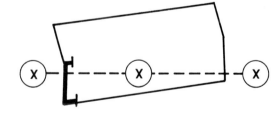

Fig. 10.55.

Stage 2:   Remain aligned to X axis (Fig. 10.56).
- Align origin point to G.
- Mark back edge and start of seam.
- Mark start of crease line.

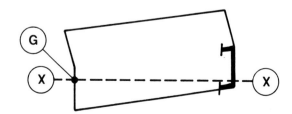

Fig. 10.56.

Stage 3: Complete seam (Fig. 10.57).
- Mark new crease line.

Fig. 10.57.

Stage 4: Align crease line of pattern to new crease line (Fig. 10.58).
- Mark underside of front edge.
- Mark start of underside seam.

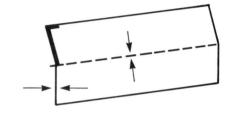

Fig. 10.58.

Stage 5: Remain aligned to crease line (Fig. 10.59).
- Move pattern along crease line until back edge touches the marked length.
- Mark underside of back edge.
- Mark start of underside seam.

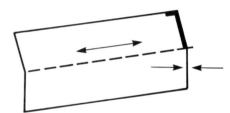

Fig. 10.59.

Stage 6: Use the pattern to complete the underside seam (Fig. 10.60).

Fig. 10.60.

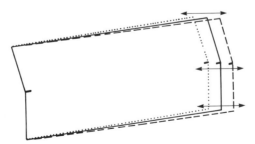

Fig. 10.61. Grade for outbreast welt.

Grading instructions:
TOP SLEEVE

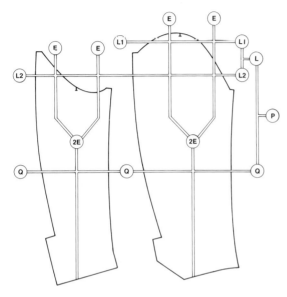

Fig. 10.62. Increments for top and under sleeves.

Increment values						
Interval	E	L	L1	L2	P	Q
4 cm	2.5	5	3	2	10	5
5 cm	3	6	4	2	12	6

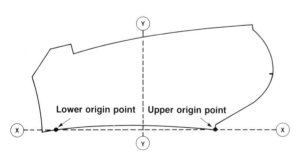

Fig. 10.63. Grading axes.

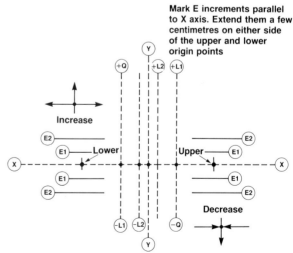

Mark E increments parallel to X axis. Extend them a few centimetres on either side of the upper and lower origin points

Fig. 10.64. Increment net.

Stage 1: Align pattern to X and Y axes (Fig. 10.65).
- Mark top half of forearm seam.
- Mark front section of sleeve head.

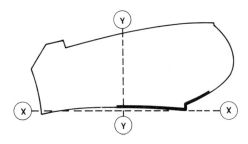

Fig. 10.65.

Stage 2: Align Y axis of pattern to Q axis on paper (Fig. 10.66).
- Align upper and lower origin points to X axis.
- Mark lower half of forearm seam.
- Mark part of cuff.

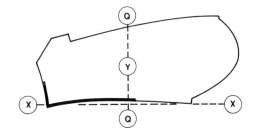

Fig. 10.66.

Stage 3: Remain aligned to Q axis (Fig. 10.67).
- Align both origin points to E2.
- Mark remainder of cuff.
- Mark vent allowance.
- Mark start of hindarm seam.

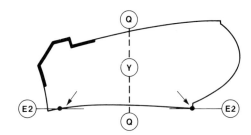

Fig. 10.67.

Stage 4: Align Y axis of pattern to L2 axis on paper (Fig. 10.68).
- Align both origin points to E2.
- Mark part of hindarm seam.
- Mark back section of sleeve head.

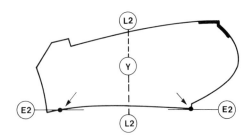

Fig. 10.68.

Stage 5: Align Y axis of pattern to L1 axis on paper (Fig. 10.69).
- Align both origin points to E1.
- Mark central section of crown.
- Mark shoulder nip.

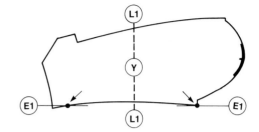

Fig. 10.69.

Stage 6: Use pattern to (Fig. 10.70):
- Complete hindarm seam.
- Blend sleeve head marks.

Fig. 10.70.

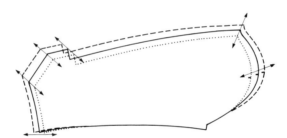

Fig. 10.71. Grade for top sleeve.

Grading instructions:
UNDER SLEEVE

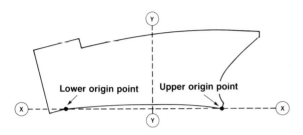

Fig. 10.72. Grading axes.

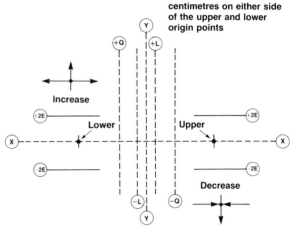

Mark E increments parallel to X axis. Extend them a few centimetres on either side of the upper and lower origin points

Fig. 10.73. Increment net.

Stage 1:   Align pattern to X and Y axes (Fig. 10.74).
* Mark top half of forearm seam.
* Mark part of underseam.

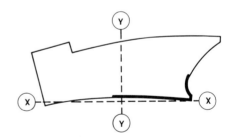

Fig. 10.74.

Stage 2:   Align Y axis of pattern to Q axis on paper (Fig. 10.75).
* Align upper and lower origin points to X axis.
* Mark lower half of forearm seam.
* Mark part of cuff.

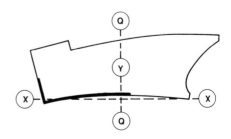

Fig. 10.75.

Stage 3: Remain aligned to Q axis (Fig. 10.76).
- Align both origin points to E2.
- Mark remainder of cuff.
- Mark vent allowance.
- Mark start of hindarm seam.

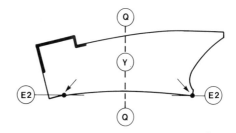

Fig. 10.76.

Stage 4: Align Y axis of pattern to L2 axis on paper (Fig. 10.77).
- Align both origin points to E2.
- Mark part of hindarm seam.
- Mark part of underseam.

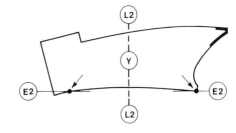

Fig. 10.77.

Stage 5: Use pattern to (Fig. 10.78):
- Complete hindarm seam.
- Blend underseam marks.

Fig. 10.78.

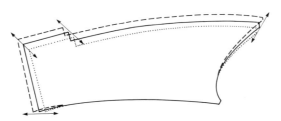

Fig. 10.79. Grade for under sleeve.

Chapter 11

Front Body Lining and Fusible Interlining for Jacket

A typically fully lined and constructed jacket could have 20 or more pattern components other than those for the top cloth, and nearly every one of these trim components has a pattern which needs to be graded. The next two examples demonstrate the grades for two major items of trim:

FRONT BODY LINING

This shows how the increments used to grade the forepart are applied to the front lining. The grade for the back and sleeve linings are exactly the same as those used for the top cloth components.

FUSIBLE INTERLINING

This grade shows a useful variation in the choice of a common origin line for the front. In this example the origin line is the section of the front edge below the first buttonhole, whereas for the top cloth front the origin line is the front side seam.

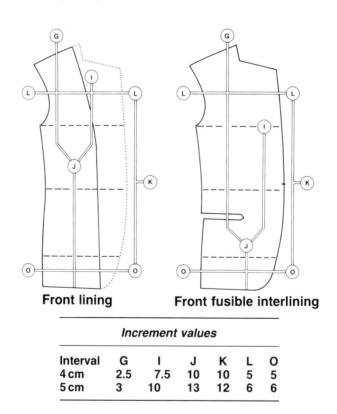

Front lining   **Front fusible interlining**

Increment values

Interval	G	I	J	K	L	O
4 cm	2.5	7.5	10	10	5	5
5 cm	3	10	13	12	6	6

Fig. 11.1. Increments for front lining and fusible interlining.

Grading instructions:
FRONT BODY LINING

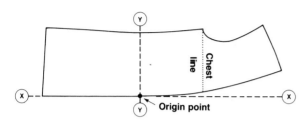

Fig. 11.2. Grading axes.

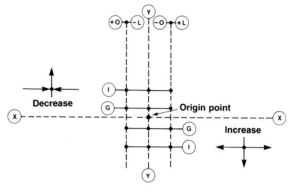

Fig. 11.3. Increment net.

Stage 1: Align the X and Y axes of the pattern and paper (Fig. 11.4).
- Mark front side seam to seat line.
- Mark part of armhole.

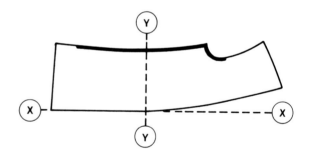

Fig. 11.4.

Stage 2: Remain aligned to X axis (Fig. 11.5).
- Align Y axis of pattern to O axis on paper.
- Complete front side seam.
- Mark part of hem.

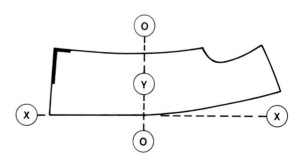

Fig. 11.5.

Stage 3:   Remain aligned to O axis (Fig. 11.6).
- Align origin point to I.
- Complete hem.
- Mark front edge to chest line.

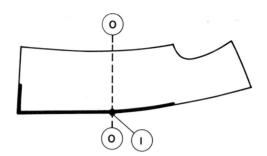

Fig. 11.6.

Stage 4:   Align front of pattern to X axis (Fig. 11.7).
- Align Y axis of pattern to L axis on paper.
- Complete armhole.
- Mark start of shoulder line.

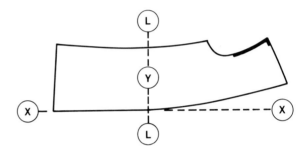

Fig. 11.7.

Stage 5:   Remain aligned to L axis (Fig. 11.8).
- Align origin point to G.
- Complete shoulder and mark corner.

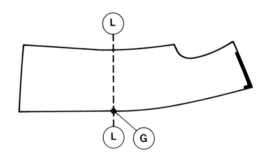

Fig. 11.8.

Stage 6:   Use pattern to (Fig. 11.9): connect the shoulder point to the front edge at the chest line.

Fig. 11.9.

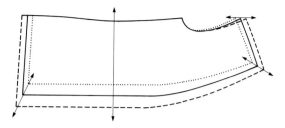

Fig. 11.10. Grade for front lining.

Grading instructions:
FUSIBLE INTERLINING

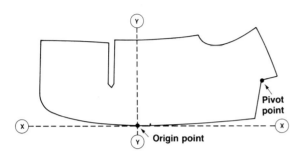

Fig. 11.11. Grading axes.

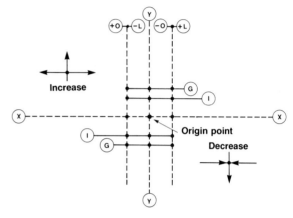

Fig. 11.12. Increment net.

Stage 1: Align X and Y axes of pattern and paper (Fig. 11.13).
- Mark a small section of button stand.
- Mark start of lapel.

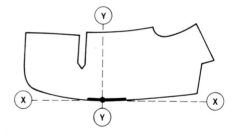

Fig. 11.13.

Stage 2: Remain on Y axis (Fig. 11.14).
- Align origin point to I.
- Mark front end of pocket cut.

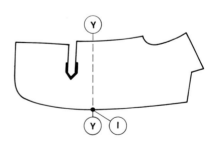

Fig. 11.14.

Stage 3: Remain on Y axis (Fig. 11.15).
- Align origin point to G.
- Complete pocket cut.
- Mark side seam from armhole to hip line.
- Mark lower section of armhole.

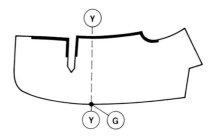

Fig. 11.15.

Stage 4: Align Y axis of pattern to O axis on paper (Fig. 11.16).
- Align origin point to G.
- Complete side seam.
- Mark part of hem.

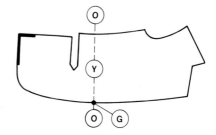

Fig. 11.16.

Stage 5: Remain on O axis (Fig. 11.17).
- Align origin point to X axis on paper.
- Complete hem and continue with cutaway to button stand.

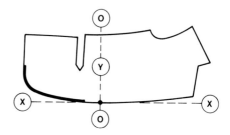

Fig. 11.17.

Stage 6: Align Y axis of pattern to L axis on paper (Fig. 11.18).
- Align origin point to I.
- Mark neck seam and corner of collar seam (pivot point).
- Mark start of shoulder.

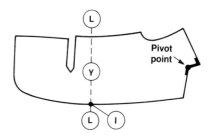

Fig. 11.18.

Stage 7: Remain on L axis (Fig. 11.19).
- Align origin point to G.
- Complete shoulder.
- Complete armhole.

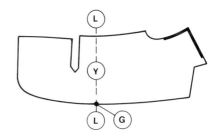

Fig. 11.19.

Stage 8: Pivot lapel from pivot point until lower edge touches line marked in Stage 1 (Fig. 11.20).
- Mark collar line, lapel step nip and lapel line.

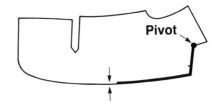

Fig. 11.20.

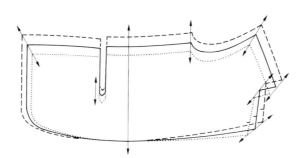

Fig. 11.21. Grade for front fusible interlining.

Chapter 12

Single Breasted Classic Waistcoat

This is a straightforward grade derived directly from that of an open necked body garment, and the demonstration grading includes the following points:

- The common origin line for the front is the edge of the button stand.
- There is an optional length grade for the section below the waist line and if used for each size the buttonhole spacings would have to be changed accordingly.

- In this demonstration the lengths of the welt pockets change from size to size by the value of increment G. Where preformed welts are used in a limited number of lengths, the welt patterns should be graded to match the standard lengths.
- The total side section grade of 2E is applied to the back only, which keeps the width of the front down to the minimum for all the sizes. This helps with materials costs because lining is generally much cheaper than top cloth.

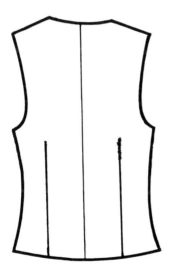

Fig. 12.1. Single breasted classic waistcoat.

Grading instructions:
WAISTCOAT FRONT

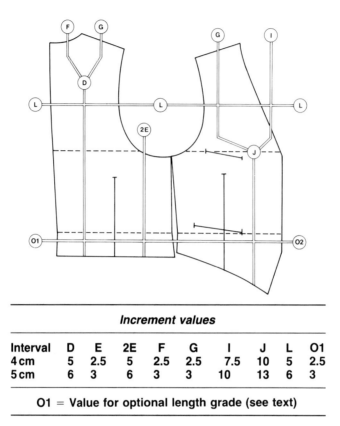

Increment values

Interval	D	E	2E	F	G	I	J	L	O1
4 cm	5	2.5	5	2.5	2.5	7.5	10	5	2.5
5 cm	6	3	6	3	3	10	13	6	3

O1 = Value for optional length grade (see text)

Fig. 12.2. Increments for single breasted classic waistcoat.

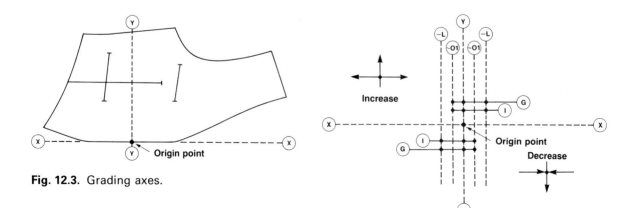

Fig. 12.3. Grading axes.

Fig. 12.4. Increment net.

Stage 1: Align the X and Y axes of the pattern and paper (Fig. 12.5).
- Mark button stand and start of neck line.

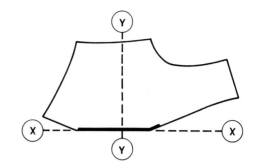

Fig. 12.5.

Stage 2: Remain on Y axis (Fig. 12.6).
- Align origin point to I.
- Mark front of pocket positions.
- Mark dart.

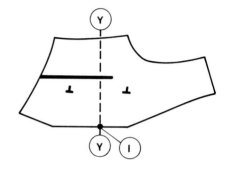

Fig. 12.6.

Stage 3: Remain on Y axis (Fig. 12.7).
- Align origin point to G.
- Mark back of pocket positions.
- Mark side seam to waist line.
- Mark lower part of armhole.

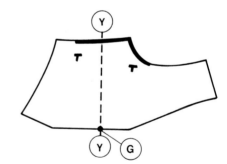

Fig. 12.7.

Stage 4: Align Y axis of pattern to O1 axis on paper (Fig. 12.8).
- Align origin point to G.
- Complete side seam.
- Mark part of bottom edge.

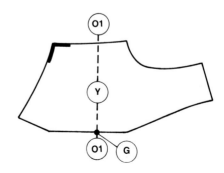

Fig. 12.8.

Stage 5: Remain aligned on O1 axis (Fig. 12.9).
- Align front edge to X axis.
- Mark cutaway, point and part of bottom edge.

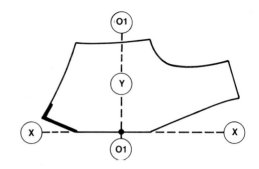

Fig. 12.9.

Stage 6: Align Y axis of pattern to L axis on paper (Fig. 12.10).
- Align origin point to I.
- Mark neck point and start of shoulder.

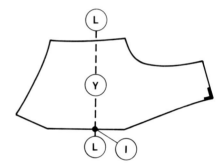

Fig. 12.10.

Stage 7: Remain aligned to L axis (Fig. 12.11).
- Align origin point to G.
- Complete shoulder line.
- Complete armhole.

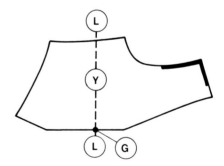

Fig. 12.11.

Stage 8: Use pattern to (Fig. 12.12):
- Join neck point to top of button stand.
- Complete and blend bottom edge.

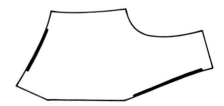

Fig. 12.12.

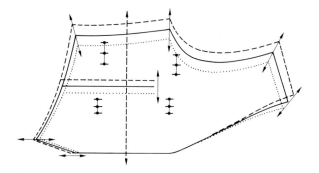

Fig. 12.13. Grade for waistcoat front incorporating optional length grade.

Grading instructions:
WAISTCOAT BACK

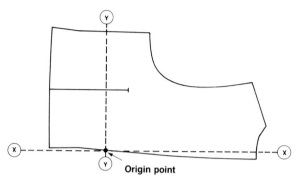

Fig. 12.14. Grading axes.

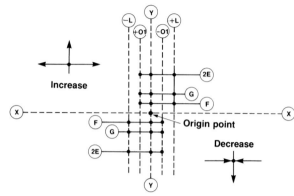

Fig. 12.15. Increment net.

Stage 1:   Align X and Y axes of pattern and paper (Fig. 12.16).
- Mark section of CB.

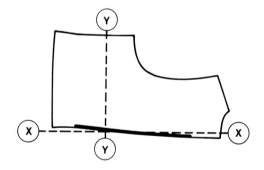

Fig. 12.16.

Stage 2:   Remain on Y axis (Fig. 12.17).
- Align origin point to G.
- Mark dart.
- Mark lower section of armhole.

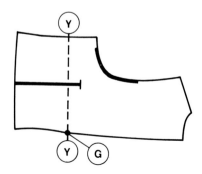

Fig. 12.17.

Stage 3: Remain on Y axis (Fig. 12.18).
- Align origin point to 2E.
- Complete lower section of armhole.
- Mark side seam to waist line.

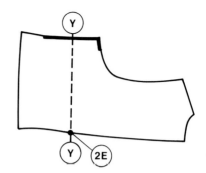

Fig. 12.18.

Stage 4: Align Y axis of pattern to O1 axis on paper (Fig. 12.19).
- Align origin point to 2E.
- Complete side seam.
- Mark part of bottom edge.

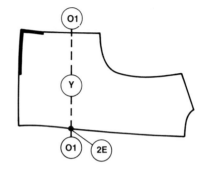

Fig. 12.19.

Stage 5: Remain on O1 axis (Fig. 12.20).
- Align origin point to X axis.
- Complete lower section of CB.
- Complete bottom edge.

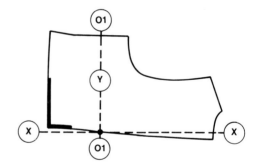

Fig. 12.20.

Stage 6: Align Y axis of pattern to L axis on paper (Fig. 12.21).
- Align origin point to X axis.
- Complete upper section of CB.
- Mark start of neck line.

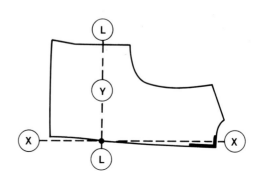

Fig. 12.21.

Stage 7: Remain on L axis (Fig. 12.22).
- Align origin point to F.
- Complete neck line.
- Mark start of shoulder.

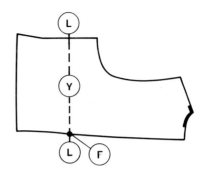

Fig. 12.22.

Stage 8: Remain on L axis (Fig. 12.23).
- Align origin point to G.
- Complete shoulder and armhole.

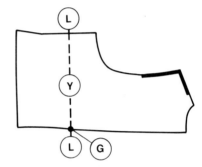

Fig. 12.23.

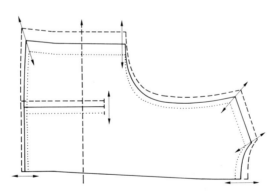

Fig. 12.24. Grade for waistcoat back incorporating optional length grade.

Chapter 13

Classic Single Breasted Overcoat with Centre Back Vent

This example is based on the basic body grade where the entire side section is attached to the forepart.

A feature of this demonstration is the method used for the proportional grading of the collar and lapel section – explained on the next page. Some other points regarding this example are:

- The common origin line for the front is the lower section of the front edge. Generally this line starts from about the waist line.
- The vent length is graded by the full value of increment O but it can also be graded proportionately or left at the same length for all the sizes.
- Pocket length is graded by the value of increment G for each size. Again, if jig sewing is used to prepare

flaps in two or three sizes only, this should be taken into account.

- Sleeves, body linings and fusibles etc. should be graded according to the principles demonstrated in Chapters 10 and 11.

Proportional grade for the collar and lapel

This method can be used when it is desirable to maintain the original base size proportions of the collar and lapel relative to the across chest and the neck to waist dimensions.

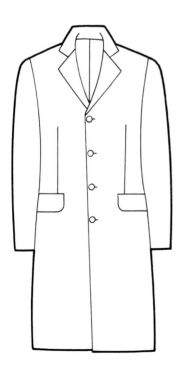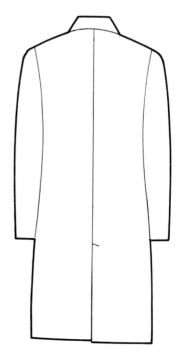

Fig. 13.1. Classic single breasted overcoat.

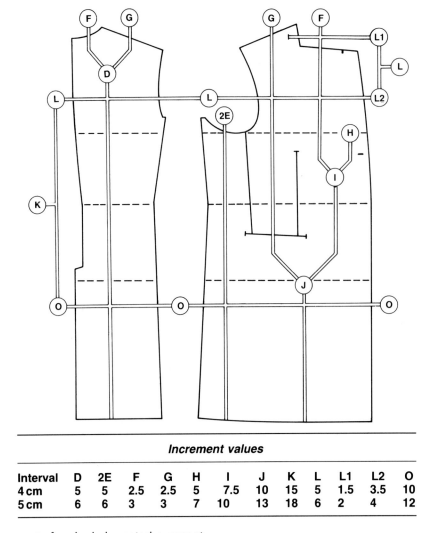

Interval	D	2E	F	G	H	I	J	K	L	L1	L2	O
4 cm	5	5	2.5	2.5	5	7.5	10	15	5	1.5	3.5	10
5 cm	6	6	3	3	7	10	13	18	6	2	4	12

Increment values

Fig. 13.2. Increments for single breasted overcoat.

LENGTH

The length proportions used are fractions of the neck to chest line grade, increment L, which is divided as follows:

L1:   This is one-third of L, applied between the front neck point and the gorge corner.
L2:   Two-thirds of L, applied between the gorge corner and the first buttonhole.

WIDTH

The lapel is graded in the width by increment F which is also used to grade the matching section of the collar.

The details of this grade are shown in Fig. 13.2. The lapel facing grade is exactly the same as that used for the matching section of the forepart.

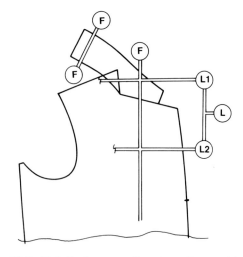

Fig. 13.3. Detail of proportionate collar and lapel grade.

Grading instructions:
OVERCOAT FRONT

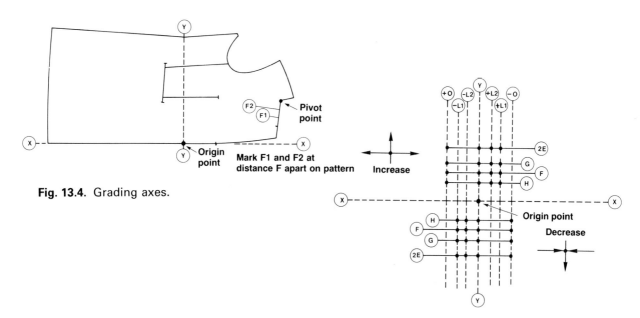

Fig. 13.4. Grading axes.

Fig. 13.5. Increment net.

Stage 1: Align the X and Y axes of the pattern and paper (Fig. 13.6).
- Mark start of lapel line.
- Mark lower section of front edge.

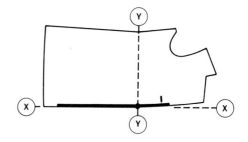

Fig. 13.6.

Stage 2: Remain on Y axis (Fig. 13.7).
- Align origin point to F.
- Mark start of pocket.
- Mark breast dart.

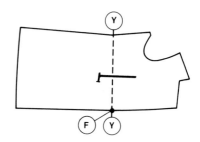

Fig. 13.7.

Stage 3: Remain on Y axis (Fig. 13.8).
● Align origin point to G.
● Mark end of pocket.
● Mark underarm dart.
● Mark lower section of armhole.

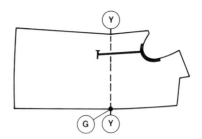

Fig. 13.8.

Stage 4: Remain on Y axis (Fig. 13.9).
● Align origin point to 2E.
● Complete lower section of armhole.
● Mark side seam to a few centimetres from the hem.

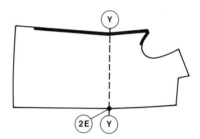

Fig. 13.9.

Stage 5: Align Y axis of pattern to O axis on paper (Fig. 13.10).
● Align front edge to X axis.
● Complete lower section of front edge and mark part of hem.

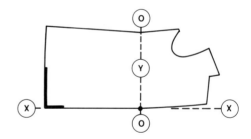

Fig. 13.10.

Stage 6: Remain on O axis (Fig. 13.11).
● Move along O axis until side seam touches the section marked in Stage 4.
● Complete side seam and hem.

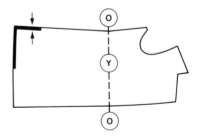

Fig. 13.11.

Stage 7: Align Y axis of pattern to L2 axis on paper (Fig. 13.12).
- Align origin point to F.
- Mark gorge corner and part of neck seam.
- Mark pivot point.

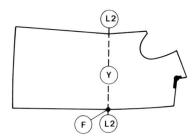

Fig. 13.12.

Stage 8: Align Y axis of pattern to L1 axis on paper (Fig. 13.13).
- Align origin point to F.
- Complete neck seam and mark start of shoulder.

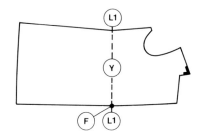

Fig. 13.13.

Stage 9: Remain aligned to L1 axis (Fig. 13.14).
- Align origin point to G.
- Complete shoulder and armhole.

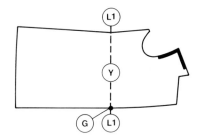

Fig. 13.14.

Stage 10: Align gorge corner of pattern to that of the size being graded (Fig. 13.15).
- Pivot the pattern from this point until the lower edge of the lapel touches the start line marked in Stage 1.
- Mark collar seam.

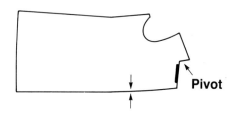

Fig. 13.15.

Stage 11A: **To increase** (Fig. 13.16)
- Mark line F1 on paper.
- Move pattern along collar seam until line F2 aligns with F1.
- Mark end of collar seam and step nip.

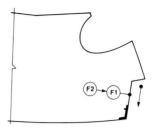

Fig. 13.16.

Stage 11B: **To decrease** (Fig. 13.17).
- Mark line F2.
- Move pattern along collar seam until line F1 aligns with F2.
- Mark end of collar seam and step nip.

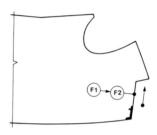

Fig. 13.17.

Stage 12: Use the pattern to join the end of the collar seam to the start of the lapel (Fig. 13.18).

Fig. 13.18.

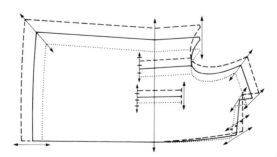

Fig. 13.19. Grade for overcoat forepart.

Grading instructions:
OVERCOAT BACK

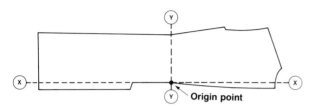

Fig. 13.20. Grading axes.

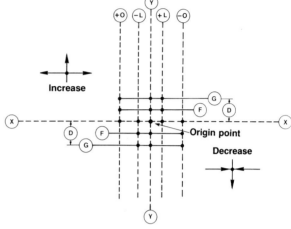

Fig. 13.21. Increment net.

Stage 1: Align X and Y axes of pattern and paper (Fig. 13.22).
- Mark part of CB and vent.

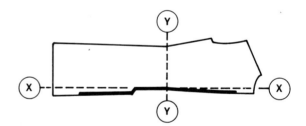

Fig. 13.22.

Stage 2: Remain on Y axis (Fig. 13.23).
- Align origin point to G.
- Mark lower section of armhole.
- Mark part of side seam to a few centimetres from the hem.

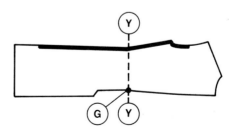

Fig. 13.23.

Stage 3: Align Y axis of pattern to O axis on paper (Fig. 13.24).
- Align origin point to X axis.
- Complete vent.
- Mark part of hem.

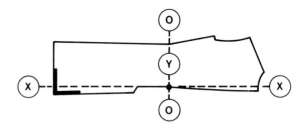

Fig. 13.24.

Stage 4: Remain on O axis (Fig. 13.25).
- Move pattern along O axis until the side seam touches the section marked in Stage 2.
- Complete side seam and hem.

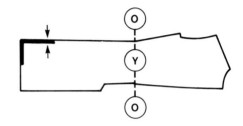

Fig. 13.25.

Stage 5: Align Y axis of pattern to L axis on paper (Fig. 13.26).
- Align origin point to X axis.
- Complete CB seam.
- Mark start of neck line.

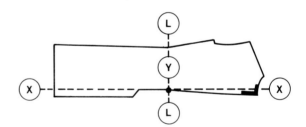

Fig. 13.26.

Stage 6: Remain on L axis (Fig. 13.27).
- Align origin point to F.
- Complete neck line.
- Mark start of shoulder.

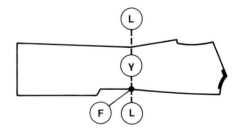

Fig. 13.27.

Stage 7: Remain on L axis (Fig. 13.28).
- Align origin point to G.
- Complete shoulder and armhole.

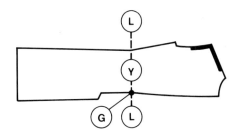

Fig. 13.28.

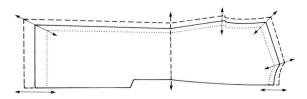

Fig. 13.29. Grade for overcoat back.

Grading instructions:
OVERCOAT COLLAR

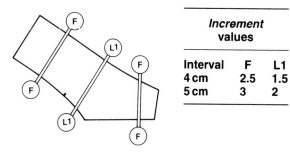

Increment values		
Interval	F	L1
4 cm	2.5	1.5
5 cm	3	2

Fig. 13.30. Grading increments for overcoat collar.

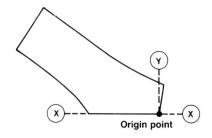

Fig. 13.31. Grading axes.

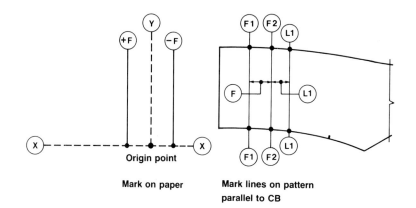

Mark on paper

Mark lines on pattern parallel to CB

Fig. 13.32. Increment nets.

Stage 1: Align seam to X axis (Fig. 13.33).
● Align origin point to Y axis.
● Mark end of collar and part of facing seam.

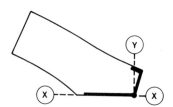

Fig. 13.33.

Stage 2:   Remain on X axis (Fig. 13.34).
- Align origin point to F.
- Mark part of outer edge.
- Mark collar heel corner and continue neck seam.

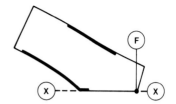

Fig. 13.34.

Stage 3A: **To increase** (Fig. 13.35).
- Mark F2 points on neck seam and outer edge.
- Move collar along neck seam until L1 points align with F2 points.
- Mark shoulder nip.

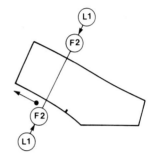

Fig. 13.35.

Stage 3B: **To decrease** (Fig. 13.36).
- Mark L1 points on neck seam and outer edge.
- Move collar along neck seam until F2 points align with L1 points.
- Mark shoulder nip.

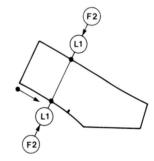

Fig. 13.36.

Stage 4A: **To increase** (Fig. 13.37).
- Remain in last position of Stage 3A.
- Mark F1 points on neck seam and outer edge.
- Move collar along neck seam until F2 points align with F1 points.
- Complete CB section of collar.

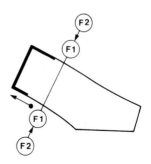

Fig. 13.37.

Stage 4B: **To decrease** (Fig. 13.38).
- Remain in last position of Stage 4A.
- Move collar along neck seam until F1 points align with the L1 points marked in Stage 4A.
- Complete CB section of collar.

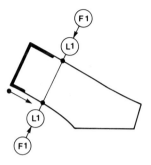

Fig. 13.38.

Stage 5:   Use pattern to blend the run of the outer edge (Fig. 13.39).

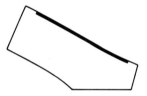

Fig. 13.39.

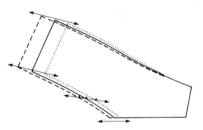

Fig. 13.40. Grade for overcoat collar.

Chapter 14

Single Breasted Top Coat with Full Raglan Sleeve

This is a classic cut garment and is often used for raincoats and overcoats. The full raglan sleeve has a number of versions and two of these are demonstrated in this example:

VERSION 1

The body has a deepened armhole with the side seam positioned at the centre of the side section and the straight sleeve split into two halves.

VERSION 2

This shows the tailored form of the raglan sleeve which can be used with a regular depth topcoat armhole. The sleeve has a split top sleeve with a regular tailored shape undersleeve. The grade for the undersleeve is the same as that shown in Chapter 10.

As the grades for the bodies for both sleeves are exactly the same, only the grade for the body with the deepened armhole is demonstrated.

Some other features of this grade are:

- The grade shows a two-way collar which can be worn buttoned up or left open as a lapel rolling to the chest line.
- The CB vent is the same length for all sizes.

Cloth belts should be graded in the length by the chest size interval.

Another version of the raglan sleeve is shown in Chapter 19.

The principle of grading raglan sleeves is to grade the sleeve section as a regular sleeve and the attached body section as the part of the body from which it was taken. In the examples the sleeve horn, which is the shoulder section of the front or back, is graded along the same axis as that used for the body. This axis is notated Z-Z and can be found by laying the start of the armhole and sleeve seams together and drawing a line on the sleeve horn parallel to the Y-Y axis used for the body.

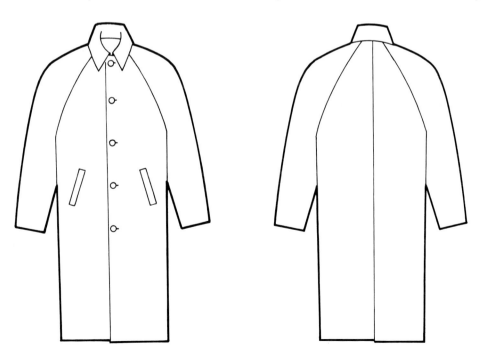

Fig. 14.1. Single breasted top coat with full raglan sleeve.

Grading instructions:
RAGLAN TOP COAT – FRONT

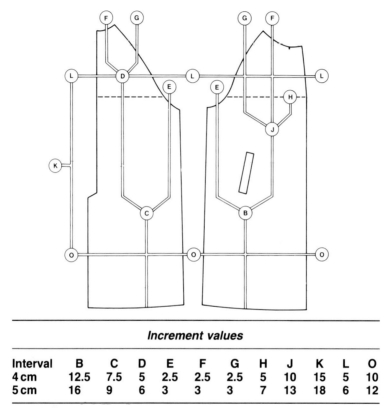

Interval	B	C	D	E	F	G	H	J	K	L	O
4 cm	12.5	7.5	5	2.5	2.5	2.5	5	10	15	5	10
5 cm	16	9	6	3	3	3	7	13	18	6	12

Increment values

Fig. 14.2. Grading increments for single breasted coat body.

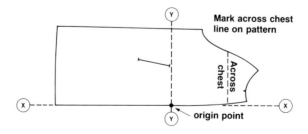

Fig. 14.3. Grading axes.

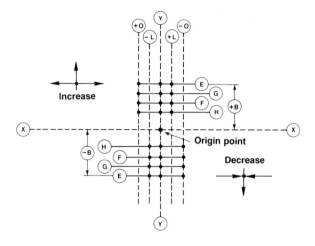

Fig. 14.4. Increment net.

Stage 1: Align X and Y axes of pattern and paper (Fig. 14.5).
- Mark part of front edge from chest line down.

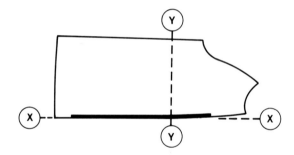

Fig. 14.5.

Stage 2: Remain on Y axis (Fig. 14.6).
- Align origin point to G.
- Mark lower section of armhole from the across chest line.
- Mark pocket position.

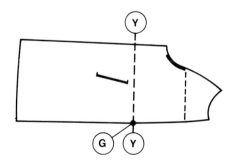

Fig. 14.6.

Stage 3:   Remain on Y axis (Fig. 14.7).
- Align origin point to E.
- Complete lower section of armhole.
- Mark section of side seam to a few centimetres
  from the hem.

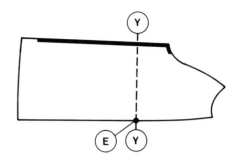

Fig. 14.7.

Stage 4:   Align Y axis of pattern to O axis on paper
(Fig. 14.8).
- Align origin point to X axis.
- Complete lower section of front edge.
- Mark part of hem.

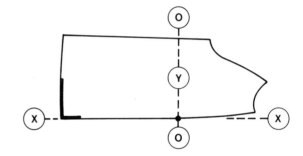

Fig. 14.8.

Stage 5:   Remain aligned to O axis (Fig. 14.9).
- Move pattern along O axis until sideseam aligns
  with section marked in Stage 3.
- Complete side seam and hem.

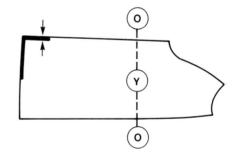

Fig. 14.9.

Stage 6:   Align Y axis of pattern to L axis on paper
(Fig. 14.10).
- Align origin point to H.
- Mark lapel step and start of neck line.

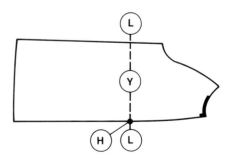

Fig. 14.10.

Stage 7: Remain on L axis (Fig. 14.11).
- Align origin point to F.
- Complete neck line.
- Mark start of armhole seam.

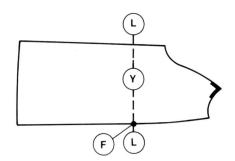

Fig. 14.11.

Stage 8: Use the pattern to (Fig. 14.12):
- Complete armhole seam.
- Join corner of the lapel step to front edge.

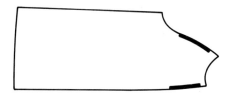

Fig. 14.12.

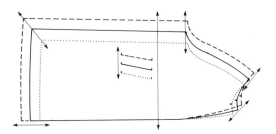

Fig. 14.13. Grade for front.

Grading instructions:
RAGLAN TOPCOAT – BACK

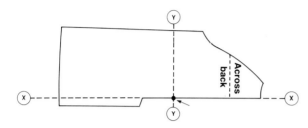

Fig. 14.14. Grading axes.

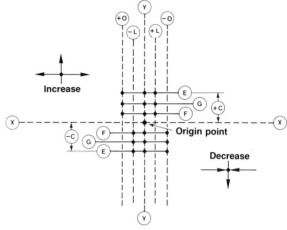

Fig. 14.15. Increment net.

Stage 1: Align X and Y axes of pattern and paper (Fig. 14.16).
- Mark part of CB.

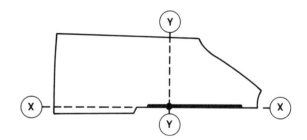

Fig. 14.16.

Stage 2: Remain aligned to Y axis (Fig. 14.17).
- Align origin point to G.
- Mark lower section of armhole from across back line.

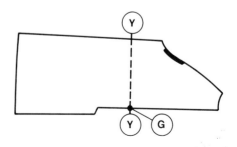

Fig. 14.17.

Stage 3: Remain aligned to Y axis (Fig. 14.18).
- Align origin point to E.
- Complete armhole.
- Mark part of side seam to a few centimetres from the hem.

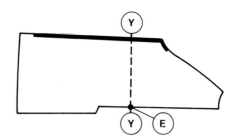

Fig. 14.18.

Stage 4: Align X axes of pattern and paper (Fig. 14.19).
- Align Y axis of pattern to O axis on paper.
- Complete CB, including the vent.
- Mark part of hem.

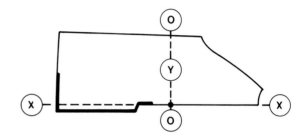

Fig. 14.19.

Stage 5: Remain on O axis (Fig. 14.20).
- Move pattern along O axis until the side seam aligns with the section marked in Stage 3.
- Complete side seam and hem.

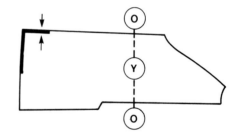

Fig. 14.20.

Stage 6: Align X axes of pattern and paper (Fig. 14.21).
- Align Y axis of pattern to L axis on paper.
- Complete upper section of CB.
- Mark start of neckline.

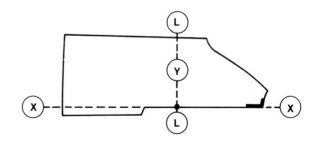

Fig. 14.21.

Stage 7: Remain aligned to L axis (Fig. 14.22).
- Align origin point to F.
- Complete neck line.
- Mark start of armhole seam.

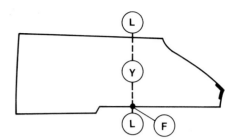

Fig. 14.22.

Stage 8: Use pattern to complete armhole seam (Fig. 14.23).

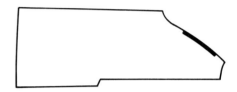

Fig. 14.23.

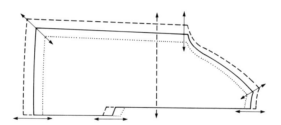

Fig. 14.24. Grade for back.

Grading instructions:
FULL RAGLAN SPLIT SLEEVE

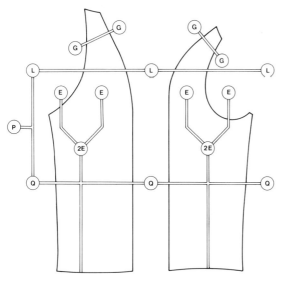

Increment values					
Interval	**E**	**G**	**L**	**P**	**Q**
4 cm	2.5	2.5	5	10	5
5 cm	3	3	6	12	6

The grades for the back and front sleeves are exactly the same.

Fig. 14.25. Grading increments for full raglan split sleeve.

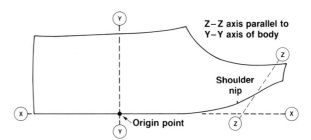

Fig. 14.26. Grading axes.

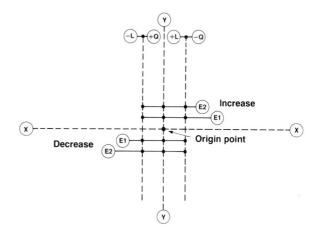

Fig. 14.27. Increment net.

The grading instructions apply similarly to the back and front sleeves.

Stage 1: Align X and Y axes of pattern and paper (Fig. 14.28).
- Mark part of overarm seam.

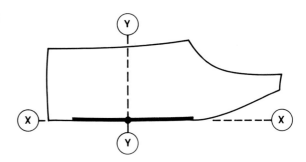

Fig. 14.28.

Stage 2: Remain on Y axis (Fig. 14.29).
- Align origin point to E1.
- Mark part of lower section of sleeve seam.

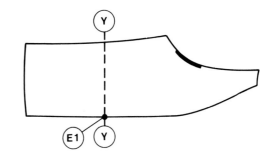

Fig. 14.29.

Stage 3: Remain on Y axis (Fig. 14.30).
- Align origin point to E2.
- Complete lower section of sleeve seam.
- Mark start of underarm seam.

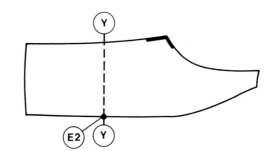

Fig. 14.30.

Stage 4: Align X axes of pattern and paper (Fig. 14.31).
- Align Y axis of pattern to Q axis on paper.
- Complete lower part of overarm seam.
- Mark part of cuff.

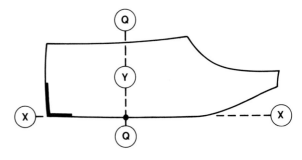

Fig. 14.31.

Stage 5: Remain on Q axis (Fig. 14.32).
- Align origin point to E2.
- Mark lower part of underarm seam.
- Complete cuff.

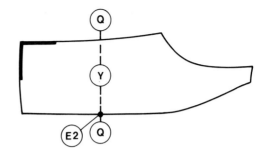

Fig. 14.32.

Stage 6: Align X axes of pattern and paper
(Fig. 14.33).
- Align Y axis of pattern to L axis on paper.
- Continue overarm seam until just past the shoulder nip.
- Mark Z-Z axis.
- Mark intersection of sleeve seam and Z-Z axis.

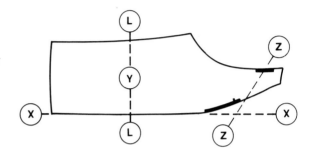

Fig. 14.33.

Stage 7: From intersection of the sleeve seam and Z-Z axis mark the value of increment G on the Z axis line (Fig. 14.34).

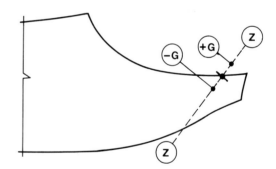

Fig. 14.34.

Stage 8: Align Z axes of pattern and paper (Fig. 14.35).
- Move pattern along Z axis until the sleeve seam touches the mark for increment G.
- Mark neck section and starts of shoulder and seam.

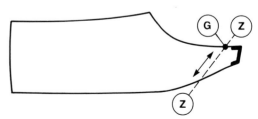

Fig. 14.35.

Stage 9: Use pattern to (Fig. 14.36):
● Connect neck point to shoulder point.
● Complete sleeve seam.
● Complete underarm seam.

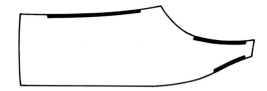

Fig. 14.36.

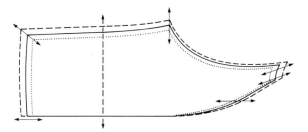

Fig. 14.37. Grade for back sleeve.

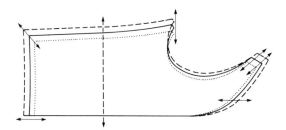

Fig. 14.38. Grade for front sleeve.

Grading instructions:
TAILORED RAGLAN SLEEVE

(A) Front top sleeve

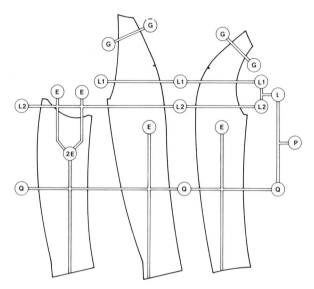

Increment values							
Interval	E	G	L	L1	L2	P	Q
4 cm	2.5	2.5	5	3	2	10	5
5 cm	3	3	6	4	2	12	6

Fig. 14.39. Grading increments for tailored raglan sleeve.

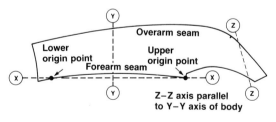

Fig. 14.40. Grading axes.

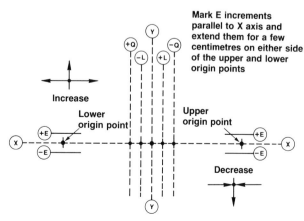

Mark E increments parallel to X axis and extend them for a few centimetres on either side of the upper and lower origin points

Fig. 14.41. Increment net.

Stage 1: Align origin points to X axis on paper (Fig. 14.42).
- Align Y axes of pattern and paper.
- Mark part of sleeve seam.
- Mark part of forearm seam.

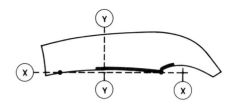

Fig. 14.42.

Stage 2: Keep origin points aligned to X axis (Fig. 14.43).
- Align Y axis of pattern to Q axis of paper.
- Complete forearm seam.
- Mark part of cuff.

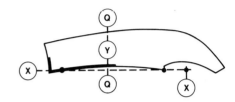

Fig. 14.43.

Stage 3: Remain aligned to Q axis (Fig. 14.44).
- Align origin points to E.
- Complete cuff.
- Mark section of overarm seam.

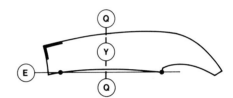

Fig. 14.44.

Stage 4: Keep origin points aligned to E (Fig. 14.45).
- Align Y axes of pattern and paper.
- Mark central section of overarm seam.

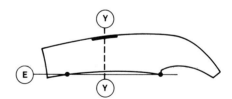

Fig. 14.45.

Stage 5: Keep origin points aligned to E (Fig. 14.46).
- Align Y axis of pattern to L axis on paper.
- Mark shoulder section of overarm seam and shoulder nip.
- Mark Z-Z axis.
- Mark intersection of Z-Z axis and sleeve seam.

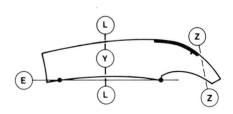

Fig. 14.46.

Stage 6: Mark value of increment G on Z axis from intersection of Z axis and sleeve seam (Fig. 14.47).

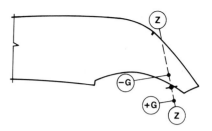

Fig. 14.47.

Stage 7: Align Z axes of pattern and paper (Fig. 14.48).
- Move pattern along Z axis until sleeve seam touches G.
- Mark neck section of sleeve horn.

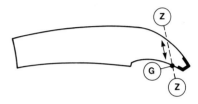

Fig. 14.48.

Stage 8: Use pattern to (Fig. 14.49):
- Complete sleeve seam.
- Complete shoulder line and overarm seam.

Fig. 14.49.

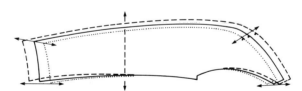

Fig. 14.50. Grade for front sleeve.

(B) Back top sleeve

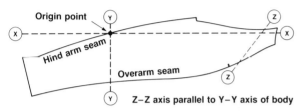

Fig. 14.51. Grading axes.

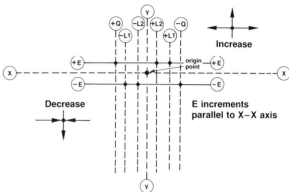

Fig. 14.52. Increment net.

Stage 1:   Align Y axes of pattern and paper
(Fig. 14.53).
- Align origin point to X axis.
- Mark central section of overarm seam.

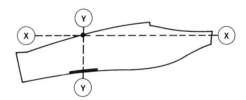

Fig. 14.53.

Stage 2:   Align Y axis of pattern to Q axis on paper
(Fig. 14.54).
- Align origin point to X axis.
- Mark lower section of overarm seam.
- Mark part of cuff.

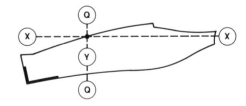

Fig. 14.54.

Stage 3:   Remain aligned to Q axis (Fig. 14.55).
- Align origin point to E.
- Complete cuff.
- Mark lower section of hindarm seam.

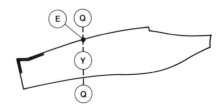

Fig. 14.55.

Stage 4: Align Y axes of pattern and paper (Fig. 14.56).
- Align origin point to E.
- Mark central section of hindarm seam.

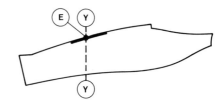

Fig. 14.56.

Stage 5: Keep origin point aligned to E (Fig. 14.57).
- Align Y axis of pattern to L2 axis on paper.
- Mark top section of hindarm seam.
- Mark start of sleeve seam.

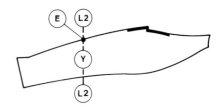

Fig. 14.57.

Stage 6: Align Y axis of pattern to L1 axis on paper (Fig. 14.58).
- Align origin point to X axis.
- Mark shoulder section of overarm seam and shoulder nip.
- Mark Z-Z axis.
- Mark intersection of Z-Z axis and sleeve seam.

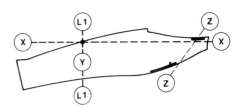

Fig. 14.58.

Stage 7: Mark value of increment G on Z axis from intersection of Z axis and sleeve seam (Fig. 14.59).

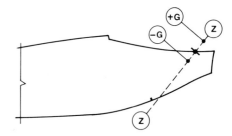

Fig. 14.59.

Stage 8: Align Z axes of pattern and paper (Fig. 14.60).
- Move pattern along Z axis until sleeve seam touches G.
- Mark neck section of sleeve horn.

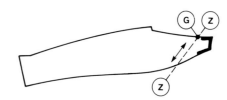

Fig. 14.60.

Stage 9: Use pattern to (Fig. 14.61):
- Complete sleeve seam.
- Complete hindarm seam.
- Complete shoulder line and overarm seam.

Fig. 14.61.

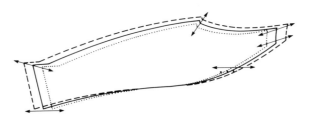

Fig. 14.62. Grade for back sleeve.

Grading instructions:
TWO-WAY COLLAR

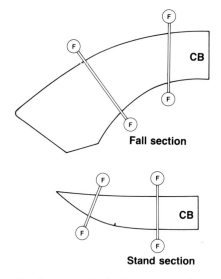

Increment value	
Interval	**F**
4 cm	**2.5**
5 cm	**3**

Fig. 14.63. Grading increments for two-way collar.

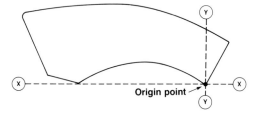

Fig. 14.64. Grading axes – fall section.

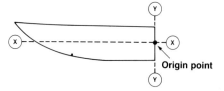

Fig. 14.65. Grading axes – stand section.

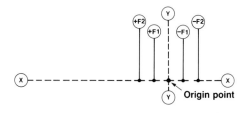

Fig. 14.66. Increment net for fall and stand sections.

FALL SECTION

Stage 1:   Align pattern to X and Y axes (Fig. 14.67).
● Mark CB section.

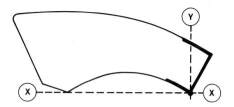

Fig. 14.67.

Stage 2:   Remain on X axis (Fig. 14.68).
● Align origin point to F1.
● Mark central section of outer edge and stand seam.

Fig. 14.68.

Stage 3:   Remain on X axis (Fig. 14.69).
● Align origin point to F2.
● Complete front section of collar.

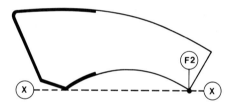

Fig. 14.69.

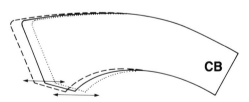

Fig. 14.70. Grade for fall section.

STAND SECTION

Stage 1: Align pattern to X and Y axes (Fig. 14.71).
● Mark CB section.

Fig. 14.71.

Stage 2: Remain on X axis (Fig. 14.72).
● Align origin point to F1.
● Mark central section of stand and neckseam.
● Mark shoulder nip.

Fig. 14.72.

Stage 3: Remain on X axis (Fig. 14.73).
● Align origin point to F2.
● Complete front section of stand and neckseam.

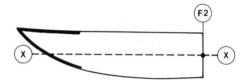

Fig. 14.73.

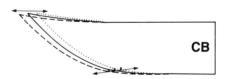

Fig. 14.74. Grade for stand section.

Chapter 15

Basic Shirt

This demonstration is of a basic long sleeved shirt with a one piece collar. The technical features of the grade are:

- The back yoke has a proportional depth grade which uses a fraction of increment L. If preferred, the yoke can remain at the same depth for all the sizes with increment L applied in its entirety through the back armhole.

- The collar length grade is derived directly from the body as is the cuff grade from the sleeve.

If the shirt has a breast patch pocket, the pocket should be graded according to the range of sizes available on the equipment used for pre-creasing or automatic setting.

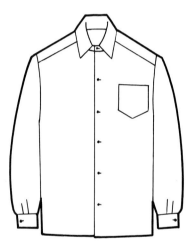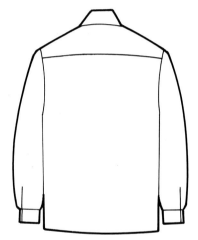

Fig. 15.1. Basic long sleeved shirt.

Grading instructions:
SHIRT FRONT

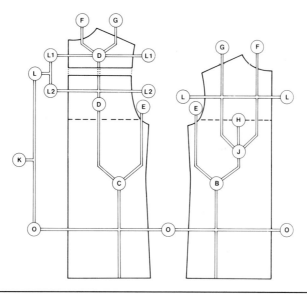

Increment values

Interval	B	C	D	E	F	G	H	J	K	L	L1	L2	O
4 cm	12.5	7.5	5	2.5	2.5	2.5	5	10	10	5	1.5	3.5	5
5 cm	16	9	6	3	3	3	7	13	12	6	2	4	6

Fig. 15.2. Increments for shirt body.

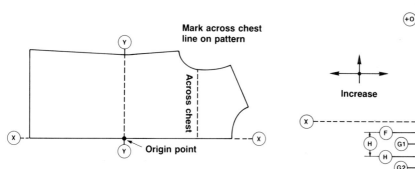

Fig. 15.3. Grading axes.

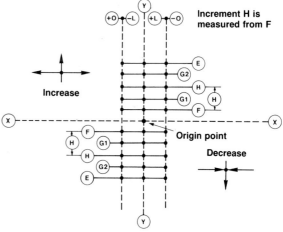

Fig. 15.4. Increment net.

Stage 1: Align X and Y axes of pattern and paper (Fig. 15.5).
- Mark part of front edge.

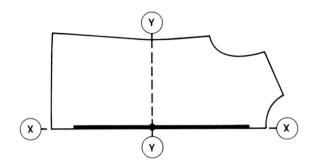

Fig. 15.5.

Stage 2: Remain aligned to Y axis (Fig. 15.6).
- Align origin point to G2.
- Mark lower section of armhole up to the across chest line.

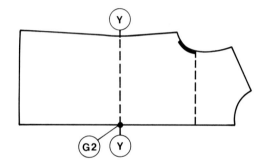

Fig. 15.6.

Stage 3: Remain on Y axis (Fig. 15.7).
- Align origin point to E.
- Complete lower section of armhole.
- Mark part of side seam.

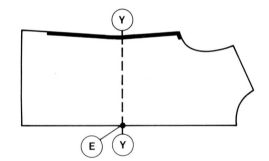

Fig. 15.7.

Stage 4: Align X axes of pattern and paper (Fig. 15.8).
- Align Y axis of pattern to O axis on paper.
- Complete lower part of front edge.
- Mark part of hem.

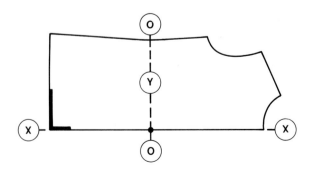

Fig. 15.8.

Stage 5:   Remain aligned to O axis (Fig. 15.9).
- Move pattern along O axis until side seam touches the section marked in Stage 3.
- Complete lower section of side seam.
- Complete hem.

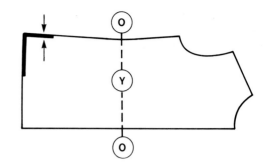

Fig. 15.9.

Stage 6:   Align X axes of pattern and paper (Fig. 15.10).
- Align Y axis of pattern to L axis on paper.
- Complete front edge.
- Mark start of neck line.

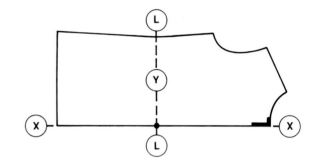

Fig. 15.10.

Stage 7:   Remain aligned to L axis (Fig. 15.11).
- Align origin point to F.
- Complete neck line.
- Mark start of shoulder.

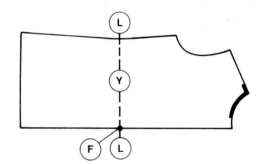

Fig. 15.11.

Stage 8:   Remain on L axis (Fig. 15.12).
- Align origin point to G1.
- Complete shoulder line.
- Mark start of armhole.

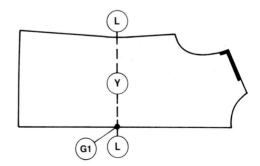

Fig. 15.12.

Stage 9: Use the pattern to blend the armhole run from the shoulder point to the across chest line. Check the armhole run with the back yoke (Fig. 15.13).

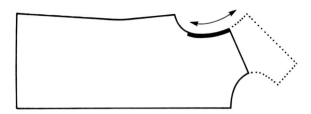

Fig. 15.13.

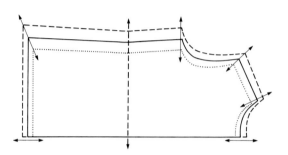

Fig. 15.14. Grade for front.

Grading instructions:
SHIRT BACK

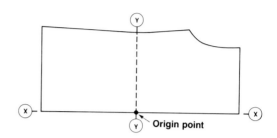

Fig. 15.15. Grading axes.

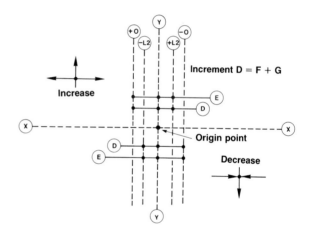

Fig. 15.16. Increment net.

Stage 1: Align X and Y axes of pattern and paper (Fig. 15.17).
• Mark part of CB.

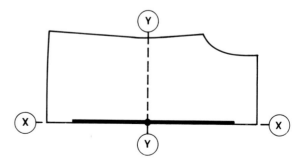

Fig. 15.17.

Stage 2:   Remain aligned to Y axis (Fig. 15.18).
- Align origin point to D.
- Mark lower section of armhole.

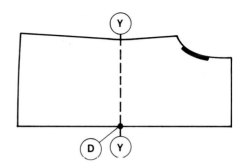

Fig. 15.18.

Stage 3:   Remain on Y axis (Fig. 15.19).
- Align origin point to E.
- Complete lower section of armhole.
- Mark part of side seam.

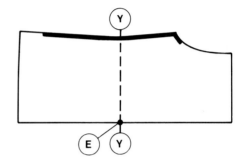

Fig. 15.19.

Stage 4:   Align X axes of pattern and paper (Fig. 15.20).
- Align Y axis of pattern to O axis on paper.
- Complete lower part of CB.
- Mark part of hem.

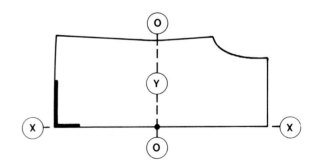

Fig. 15.20.

Stage 5:   Remain aligned to O axis (Fig. 15.21).
- Move pattern along O axis until the side seam touches the part marked in Stage 3.
- Complete side seam and hem.

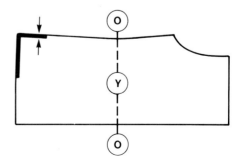

Fig. 15.21.

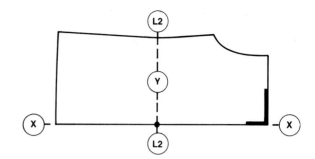

Stage 6: Align X axes of pattern and paper (Fig. 15.22).
- Align Y axis of pattern to L2 axis on paper.
- Complete CB.
- Mark part of yoke seam.

Fig. 15.22.

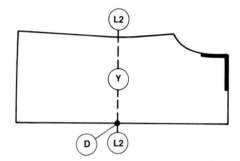

Stage 7: Remain aligned to L2 axis (Fig. 15.23).
- Align origin point to D.
- Complete yoke seam and armhole.

Fig. 15.23.

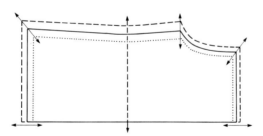

Fig. 15.24.

Grading instructions:
SHIRT YOKE

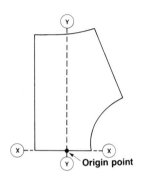

Fig. 15.25. Grading axes for yoke.

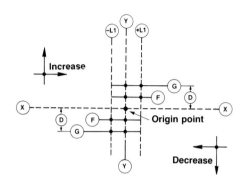

Fig. 15.26. Increment net.

Stage 1: Align X and Y axes of pattern and paper (Fig. 15.27).
- Mark part of CB.
- Mark part of yoke seam.

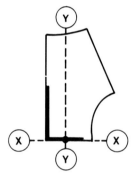

Fig. 15.27.

Stage 2: Remain aligned to Y axis (Fig. 15.28).
- Align origin point to G (also = D).
- Complete yoke seam.
- Mark part of armhole.

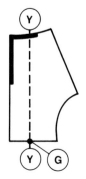

Fig. 15.28.

Stage 3: Align X axes of pattern and paper
(Fig. 15.29).
- Align Y axis of pattern to L1 axis on paper.
- Complete CB.
- Mark start of neckline.

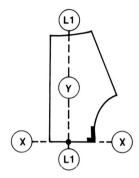

Fig. 15.29.

Stage 4: Remain aligned to L1 axis (Fig. 15.30).
- Align origin point to F.
- Complete neck line.
- Mark start of shoulder.

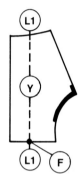

Fig. 15.30.

Stage 5: Remain on L1 axis (Fig. 15.31).
- Align origin point to G.
- Complete shoulder and armhole.

Fig. 15.31.

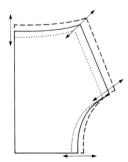

Fig. 15.32. Grade for yoke.

Grading instructions:
SHIRT SLEEVE

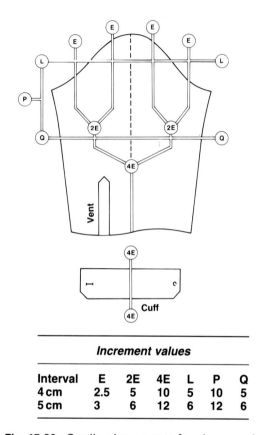

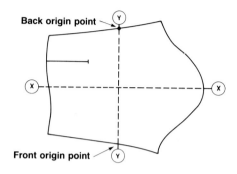

Fig. 15.34. Grading axes.

Increment values						
Interval	E	2E	4E	L	P	Q
4 cm	2.5	5	10	5	10	5
5 cm	3	6	12	6	12	6

Fig. 15.33. Grading increments for sleeve and cuff.

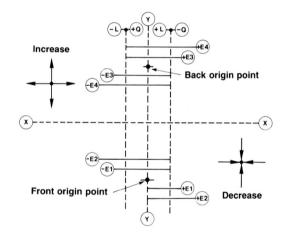

Fig. 15.35. Increment net.

Stage 1: Align X axes of pattern and paper (Fig. 15.36).
- Align Y axis of pattern to L axis on paper.
- Mark vertex of sleeve head.

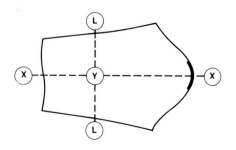

Fig. 15.36.

Stage 2: Align Y axes of pattern and paper (Fig. 15.37).
- Align front origin point to E1.
- Mark part of front sleeve head.

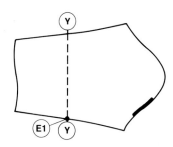

Fig. 15.37.

Stage 3: Remain on Y axis (Fig. 15.38).
- Align front origin point to E2.
- Mark under section of sleeve head and start of underarm seam.

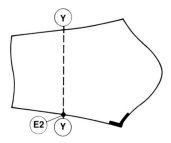

Fig. 15.38.

Stage 4: Remain on Y axis (Fig. 15.39).
- Align back origin point to E3.
- Mark part of back sleeve head.

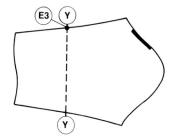

Fig. 15.39.

Stage 5: Remain on Y axis (Fig. 15.40).
- Align back origin point to E4.
- Mark under section of sleeve head and start of underarm seam.

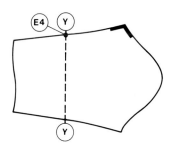

Fig. 15.40.

Stage 6: Align Y axis of pattern to Q axis on paper (Fig. 15.41).
- Align front origin point to E2.
- Mark end of front underarm seam and part of cuff.

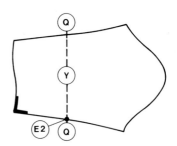

Fig. 15.41.

Stage 7: Remain on Q axis (Fig. 15.42).
- Align front origin point to E1.
- Complete front half of cuff.

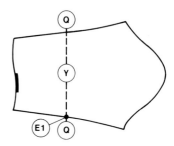

Fig. 15.42.

Stage 8: Remain on Q axis (Fig. 15.43).
- Align back origin point to E3.
- Mark part of cuff.
- Mark sleeve vent.

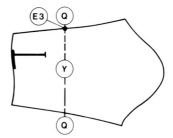

Fig. 15.43.

Stage 9: Remain on Q axis (Fig. 15.44).
- Align back origin point to E4.
- Complete back half of cuff.
- Mark end of back underarm seam.

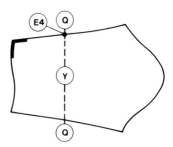

Fig. 15.44.

Stage 10: Use pattern to (Fig. 15.45):
- Complete underarm seams.
- Blend sleeve head.

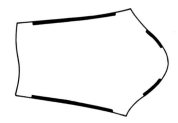

Fig. 15.45.

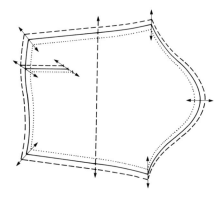

Fig. 15.46. Grade for sleeve.

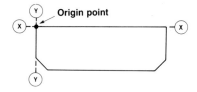

Fig. 15.47. Grading axes for cuff.

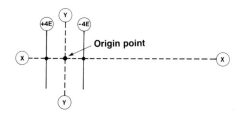

Fig. 15.48. Increment net.

Increase or decrease cuff
length at one end by 4E

Fig. 15.49. Grade for cuff.

Grading instructions:
SHIRT COLLAR

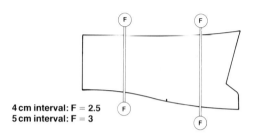

Fig. 15.50. Grading increments for collar.

4 cm interval: F = 2.5
5 cm interval: F = 3

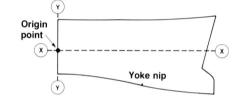

Fig. 15.51. Grading axes.

Origin point

Yoke nip

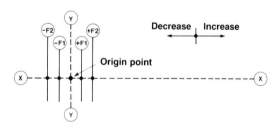

Fig. 15.52. Increment net.

−F2 −F1 +F1 +F2

Decrease Increase

Origin point

Stage 1: Align X and Y axes of pattern and paper (Fig. 15.53).
- Mark CB section of collar.

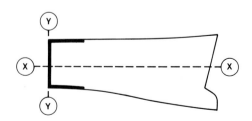

Fig. 15.53.

Stage 2: Remain on X axis (Fig. 15.54).
- Align origin point to F1.
- Mark central section of outer edge and neck seam.
- Mark yoke nip.

Fig. 15.54.

Stage 3: Remain on X axis (Fig. 15.55).
- Align origin point to F2.
- Complete collar.

Fig. 15.55.

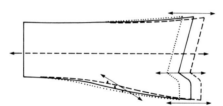

Fig. 15.56. Grade for collar.

Chapter 16

Tuxedo Jacket Forepart with Shawl Collar

The highlight of this grade for a single breasted, button one shawl collar tuxedo is the method used to maintain the lapel section shape and length proportions for all the sizes.

The break line, also called the crease row, is used during the grade as an axis for controlling the lapel section width and length. This jacket has a one-piece facing and its grade is derived directly from the relevant sections of the body and undercollar. The back neck sections of the neck piece and under collar are both graded in the length by the selected value for increment F.

In this example, only the grade for the forepart, facing, neck piece and under collar are shown and the rest of the body should be graded in the same way as those demonstrated in Grade 6.1.

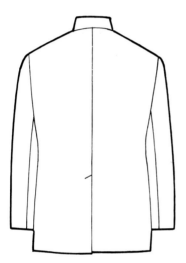

Fig. 16.1. Tuxedo jacket forepart with shawl collar.

Grading instructions:
TUXEDO FOREPART

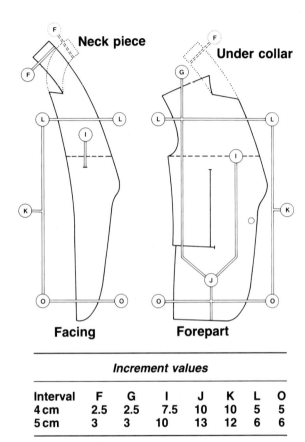

Facing   **Forepart**

Increment values							
Interval	F	G	I	J	K	L	O
4 cm	2.5	2.5	7.5	10	10	5	5
5 cm	3	3	10	13	12	6	6

Fig. 16.2. Grading increments for forepart and facing.

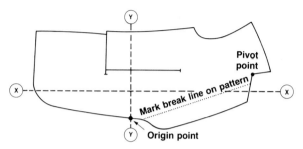

Fig. 16.3. Grading axes.

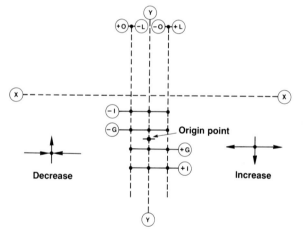

Fig. 16.4. Increment net.

Stage 1: Align X and Y axes of pattern and paper (Fig. 16.5).
- Mark part of front side seam and lower section of armhole.
- Mark start of pocket dart.

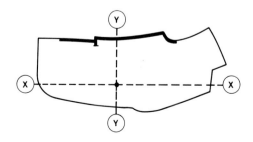

Fig. 16.5.

Stage 2: Remain aligned to Y axis (Fig. 16.6).
- Align origin point to G.
- Complete pocket dart.
- Mark breast dart.

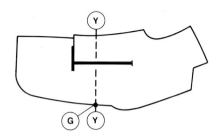

Fig. 16.6.

Stage 3: Remain on Y axis (Fig. 16.7).
- Align origin point to I.
- Mark break point and end of break line.
- Mark start of cutaway line.

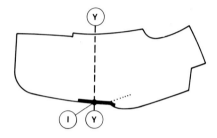

Fig. 16.7.

Stage 4: Align Y axis of pattern to O axis on paper (Fig. 16.8).
- Align origin point to I.
- Mark lower section of cutaway line and part of hem.

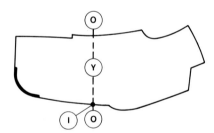

Fig. 16.8.

Stage 5: Remain aligned to O axis (Fig. 16.9).
- Move pattern along O axis until front side seam touches line marked in Stage 1.
- Complete front side seam.
- Complete hem.

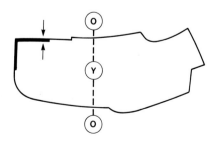

Fig. 16.9.

Stage 6:   Align X axes of pattern and paper
(Fig. 16.10).
- Align Y axis of pattern to L axis on paper.
- Complete armhole and mark shoulder end.

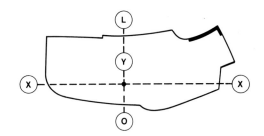

Fig. 16.10.

Stage 7:   Remain aligned to L axis (Fig. 16.11).
- Align origin point to G.
- Complete shoulder.
- Mark gorge seam and pivot point.
- Mark start of break line.

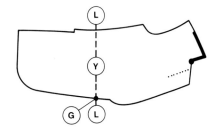

Fig. 16.11.

Stage 8:   On the paper connect the start and end of the
break line, which will be in a different position for each
size (Fig. 16.12).

Fig. 16.12.

Stage 9:   Use an awl to align the pivot point of the
pattern to that marked on the paper (Fig. 16.13).
- Pivot the pattern from this point until the breakline
  on the pattern aligns with that on the paper.
- Mark collar seam and top section of lapel.

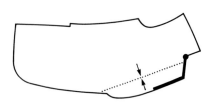

Fig. 16.13.

Stage 10:   Release awl but keep the break lines in
alignment (Fig. 16.14).
- Move the pattern along the new break line until the
  end of the pattern break line aligns with the section
  marked in Stage 3.
- Complete lapel.

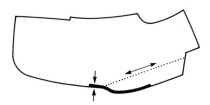

Fig. 16.14.

Stage 11: Use pattern to complete the cutaway line
(Fig. 16.15).

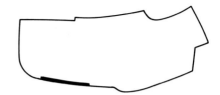

Fig. 16.15.

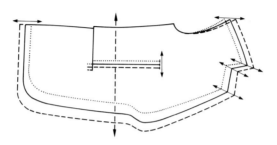

Fig. 16.16. Grade for front.

Grading instructions:
TUXEDO FACING

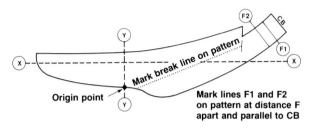

Fig. 16.17. Grading axes.

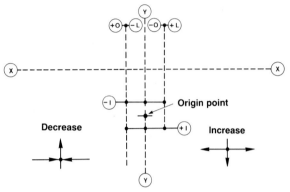

Fig. 16.18. Increment net.

Stage 1: Align Y axes of pattern and paper (Fig. 16.19).
- Align origin point to I.
- Mark start of cutaway line.
- Mark break point and end of break line.
- Mark part of inside edge.

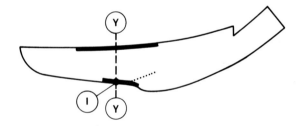

Fig. 16.19.

Stage 2: Align Y axis of pattern to O axis on paper (Fig. 16.20).
- Align origin point to I.
- Mark end section of facing.

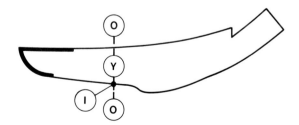

Fig. 16.20.

Stage 3: Align X axes of pattern and paper
(Fig. 16.21).
- Align Y axis of pattern to L axis on paper.
- Mark shoulder section of facing.
- Mark pivot point.
- Mark start of break line.

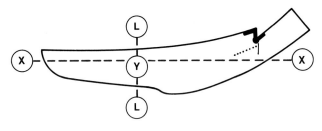

Fig. 16.21.

Stage 4: On the paper, connect the start and end of
the break line, which will be in a different position for
each size (Fig. 16.22).

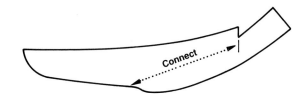

Fig. 16.22.

Stage 5: Use an awl to align the pivot point of the
pattern to that marked on the paper (Fig. 16.23).
- Pivot the pattern from this point until the break line
  on the pattern aligns with that on the paper.
- Mark neck seam and upper section of facing.
- **To increase**: Mark line F1.
- **To decrease**: Mark line F2.

Fig. 16.23.

Stage 6: Release the awl but keep the break lines in
alignment (Fig. 16.24).
- Move the pattern along the new break line until the
  end of the pattern break line aligns with the section
  marked in Stage 1.
- Complete the lapel.

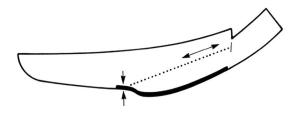

Fig. 16.24.

Stage 7a: **To increase** (Fig. 16.25).
- Move pattern along neck seam until line F2 aligns with line F1.
- Complete CB section of facing.

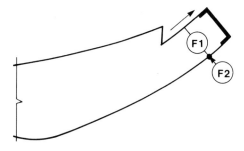

Fig. 16.25.

Stage 7b: **To decrease** (Fig. 16.26).
- Move pattern along neck seam until line F1 aligns with line F2.
- Complete CB section of facing.

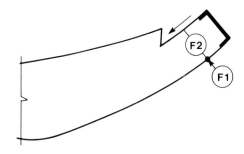

Fig. 16.26.

Stage 8: Use pattern to (Fig. 16.27).
- Complete inside edge.
- Complete the cutaway line.

Fig. 16.27.

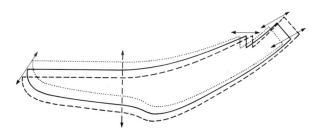

Fig. 16.28. Grade for facing.

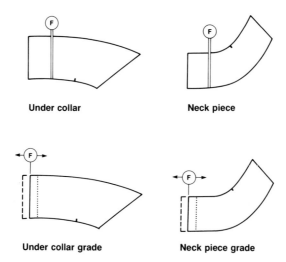

Under collar   Neck piece

Under collar grade   Neck piece grade

Fig. 16.29. Under collar and neck piece: increase or decrease the back neck length by the selected value of increment F.

Chapter 17

Waistcoat with Half Collar

This is an example of the grade for a styled waistcoat with a one-piece lapel and collar which is sandwiched on to the front between the top buttonhole and the shoulder. The collar section ends at the shoulder line.

The front grade is exactly the same as that for the basic waistcoat (Chapter 12) but in this demonstration, as an alternative method, the side seam is the common origin line.

The back grade is also the same as that demonstrated in Chapter 12.

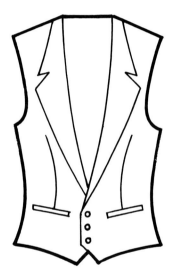 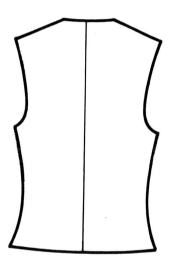

Fig. 17.1. Waistcoat with half collar.

Grading instructions:
WAISTCOAT FRONT

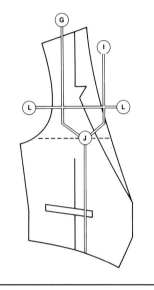

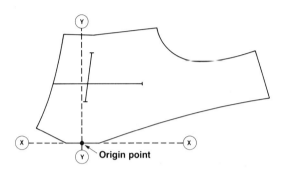

Fig. 17.3. Grading axes.

Increment values

Interval	G	I	J	L
4 cm	2.5	7.5	10	5
5 cm	3	10	13	6

Fig. 17.2. Grading increments for front and lapel.

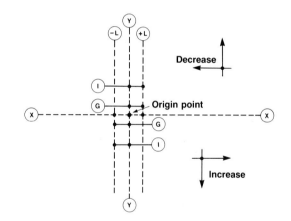

Fig. 17.4. Increment net.

Stage 1: Align X and Y axes of pattern and paper (Fig. 17.5).
- Mark lower section of armhole.
- Mark side seam.
- Mark start of hem.
- Mark back of pocket position.

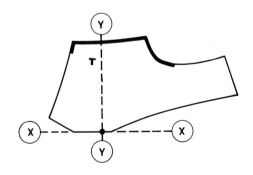

Fig. 17.5.

Stage 2: Remain on Y axis (Fig. 17.6).
- Align origin point to G.
- Mark front end of pocket.
- Mark breast dart.
- Mark central section of hem.

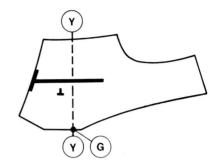

Fig. 17.6.

Stage 3: Remain on Y axis (Fig. 17.7).
- Align origin point to I.
- Mark corner and part of hem.
- Mark button stand and start of lapel seam.

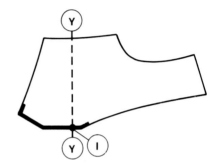

Fig. 17.7.

Stage 4: Align X axes of pattern and paper
(Fig. 17.8).
- Align Y axis of pattern to L axis on paper.
- Mark upper section of armhole and end of shoulder line.

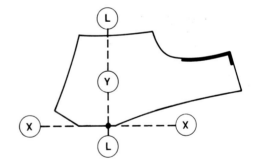

Fig. 17.8.

Stage 5: Remain on L axis (Fig. 17.9).
- Align origin point to G.
- Complete shoulder.
- Mark start of lapel seam.

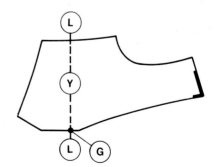

Fig. 17.9.

Stage 6: Use pattern to (Fig. 17.10):
- Blend hem line.
- Join neck point to button stand.

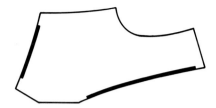

Fig. 17.10.

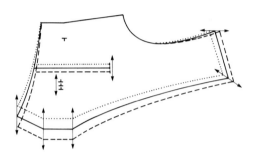

Fig. 17.11. Grade for front.

Grading instructions:
LAPEL AND COLLAR SECTION

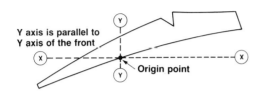

Fig. 17.12. Grading axes for lapel and collar section.

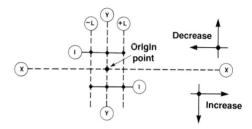

Fig. 17.13. Increment net.

Stage 1: Align Y axes of pattern and paper (Fig. 17.14).
- Align origin point to I.
- Mark end of lapel.

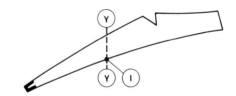

Fig. 17.14.

Stage 2: Align Y axis of pattern to L axis on paper (Fig. 17.15).
- Align origin point to X axis.
- Mark shoulder line section of collar.

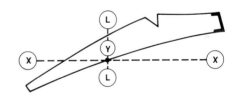

Fig. 17.15.

Stage 3: Use the pattern to connect the seam line from the shoulder to the end (Fig. 17.16).

Fig. 17.16.

Stage 4: Mark the value of $\frac{L}{2}$ from the intersection of the shoulder line and seam (Fig. 17.17).
- **To increase**: Mark below shoulder line.
- **To decrease**: Mark above shoulder line.

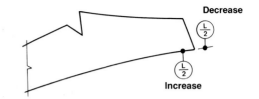

Fig. 17.17.

Stage 5: Align the seam line of the pattern to the seam line marked in Stage 3 (Fig. 17.18).
- Align front neck point to the relevant $\frac{L}{2}$ mark.
- Complete lapel and collar lines.

Fig. 17.18.

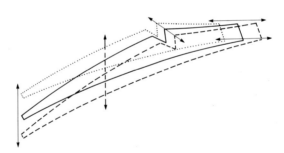

Fig. 17.19. Grade for lapel and collar section.

Chapter 18

Anorak with Attached Hood

The style features of this garment include an attached hood, an all round yoke, and a waist that could be elasticated or could have an inserted draw string. The armhole has been deepened.

A technical aspect of this grade is the application of increment H in two stages:

Stage 1: From the centre front neck point to the yoke line.
Stage 2: From the yoke line to the chest line and then downwards, parallel to the front edge.

Obviously the demonstration of this grade cannot give the sub-divisions of increment H because the values involved are a function of the size interval being graded and the position of the yoke line on the centre front of the anorak.

Fig. 18.2 shows these applications and the values can be established very simply by adding increment H to the chest line at the centre front and connecting it to the centre front neck point. The values of H2 and H3 can be measured off from where the yoke line intersects the triangle formed by the addition of H at the chest line.

Another aspect of this grade is that the armhole depth grade of increment L is applied proportionately between the yoke and the body. The division is notated $\frac{L}{2}$ on the respective increment nets.

Fig. 18.1. Anorak with attached hood.

182

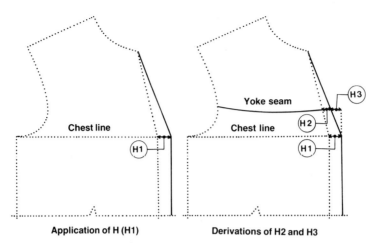

Fig. 18.2. Front yoke and increment H.

Grading instructions:
ANORAK FRONT

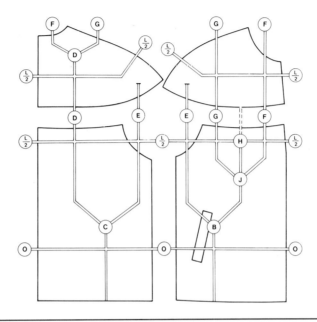

Increment values

Interval	B	C	D	E	F	G	H	J	Length = L + O	L	$\frac{L}{2}$	O
4 cm	12.5	7.5	5	2.5	2.5	2.5	5	10	10	5	2.5	5
5 cm	16	9	6	3	3	3	7	13	12	6	3	6

Fig. 18.3. Increments for anorak body.

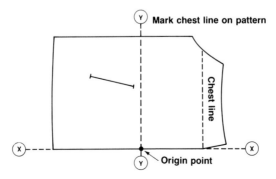

Fig. 18.4. Grading axes for front.

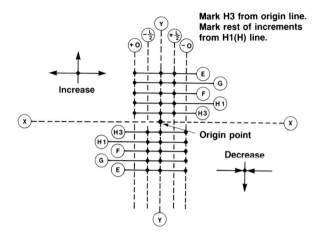

Mark H3 from origin line.
Mark rest of increments
from H1(H) line.

Fig. 18.5. Increment net.

Stage 1: Align pattern to X and Y axes (Fig. 18.6).
● Mark part of CF from chest line down.

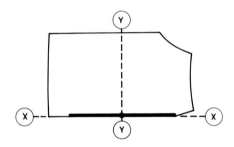

Fig. 18.6.

Stage 2: Remain on Y axis (Fig. 18.7).
● Align origin point to G.
● Mark pocket position.
● Mark part of armhole.

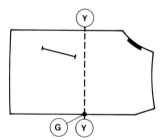

Fig. 18.7.

Stage 3: Remain on Y axis (Fig. 18.8).
● Align origin point to E.
● Mark centre of armhole.
● Mark part of side seam.

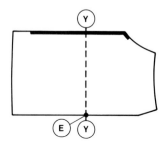

Fig. 18.8.

Stage 4: Align X axes of pattern and paper
(Fig. 18.9).
- Align Y axis of pattern to O axis on paper.
- Complete lower section of CF.
- Mark part of hem.

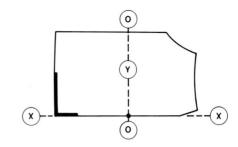

Fig. 18.9.

Stage 5: Remain aligned to O axis (Fig. 18.10).
- Move pattern along O axis until the side seam
  aligns with the mark made in Stage 3.
- Complete side seam and hem.

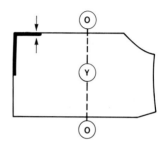

Fig. 18.10.

Stage 6: Align Y axis of pattern to $\frac{L}{2}$ axis on paper
(Fig. 18.11).
- Align origin point to H3.
- Mark corner of CF and yoke seam.

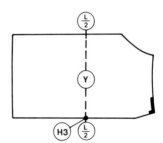

Fig. 18.11.

Stage 7: Remain on $\frac{L}{2}$ axis (Fig. 18.12).

- Align origin point to G.
- Mark part of yoke seam and complete armhole.

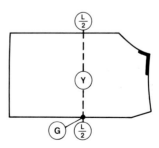

Fig. 18.12.

Stage 8: Use pattern to (Fig. 18.13):
- Blend the yoke seam.
- Join the CF corner of the yoke seam to the chest line.

Fig. 18.13.

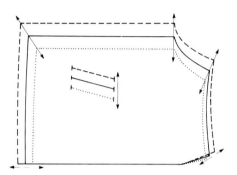

Fig. 18.14. Grade for front.

Grading instructions:
FRONT YOKE

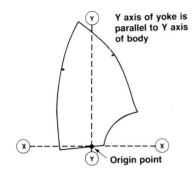

Fig. 18.15. Grading axes for front yoke.

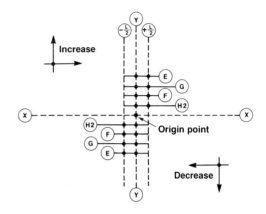

Fig. 18.16. Increment net.

Stage 1: Align pattern to X and Y axes (Fig. 18.17).
- Mark corner of CF and yoke seam.

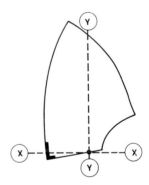

Fig. 18.17.

Stage 2: Remain on Y axis (Fig. 18.18).
- Align origin point to G.
- Mark part of yoke seam.
- Mark armhole seam nip.

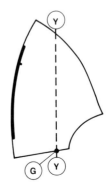

Fig. 18.18.

188

Stage 3: Remain on Y axis (Fig. 18.19).
- Align origin point to E.
- Mark sleeve section of yoke seam and corner with shoulder seam.

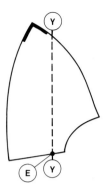

Fig. 18.19.

Stage 4: Align Y axis of pattern to $\frac{L}{2}$ axis on paper (Fig. 18.20).
- Align origin point to H2.
- Mark corner of CF and start of neck line.

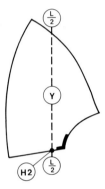

Fig. 18.20.

Stage 5: Remain on $\frac{L}{2}$ axis (Fig. 18.21).
- Align origin point to F.
- Complete neck line.
- Mark start of shoulder line.

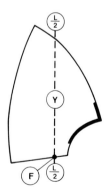

Fig. 18.21.

Stage 6: Remain on $\frac{L}{2}$ axis (Fig. 18.22).

- Align origin point to G.
- Complete shoulder line.
- Mark shoulder nip.
- Mark part of overarm seam.

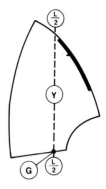

Fig. 18.22.

Stage 7: Use pattern to (Fig. 18.23):
- Complete overarm seam.
- Join CF neck point to start of yoke seam.

Fig. 18.23.

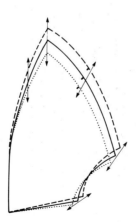

Fig. 18.24. Grade for front yoke.

Grading instructions:
ANORAK BACK

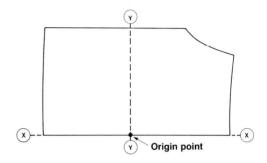

Fig. 18.25. Grading axes for back.

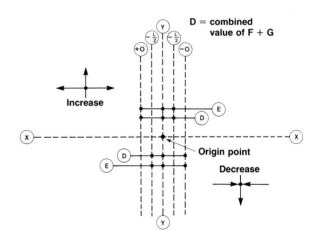

Fig. 18.26. Increment net.

Stage 1: Align X and Y axes of pattern and paper (Fig. 18.27).
- Mark part of CB.

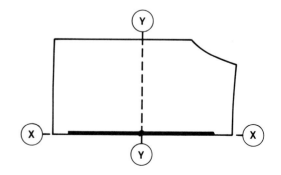

Fig. 18.27.

Stage 2:   Remain on Y axis (Fig. 18.28).
- Align origin point to D.
- Mark part of armhole.

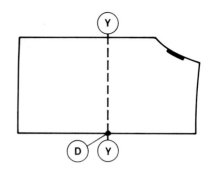

Fig. 18.28.

Stage 3:   Remain on Y axis (Fig. 18.29).
- Align origin point to E.
- Complete lower section of armhole.
- Mark part of side seam.

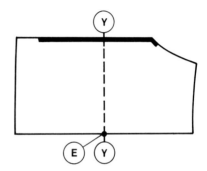

Fig. 18.29.

Stage 4:   Align X axes of pattern and paper (Fig. 18.30).
- Align Y axis of pattern to O axis on paper.
- Complete lower section of CB.
- Mark part of hem.

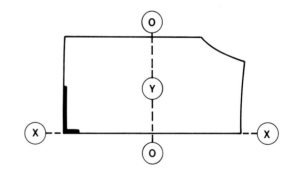

Fig. 18.30.

Stage 5: Remain on O axis (Fig. 18.31).
- Move pattern along O axis until the side seam touches the line marked in Stage 3.
- Complete side seam and hem.

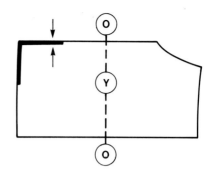

Fig. 18.31.

Stage 6: Align X axes of pattern and paper (Fig. 18.32).
- Align Y axis of pattern to $\frac{L}{2}$ axis on paper.
- Complete CB.
- Mark start of yoke seam.

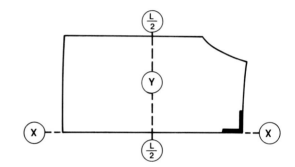

Fig. 18.32.

Stage 7: Remain on $\frac{L}{2}$ axis (Fig. 18.33).
- Align origin point to D.
- Complete yoke seam.
- Mark start of armhole.

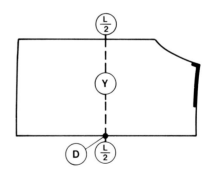

Fig. 18.33.

Stage 8:   Use pattern to blend armhole line
(Fig. 18.34).

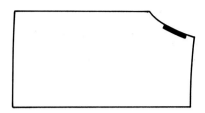

Fig. 18.34.

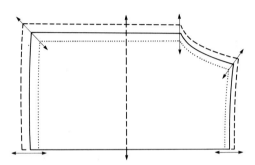

Fig. 18.35. Grade for back.

Grading instructions:
BACK YOKE

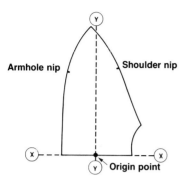

Fig. 18.36. Grading axes for back yoke.

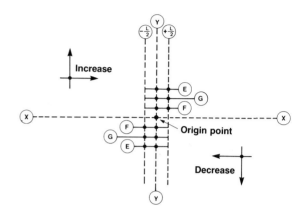

Fig. 18.37. Increment net.

Stage 1: Align X and Y axes of pattern and paper (Fig. 18.38).
- Mark part of CB.
- Mark start of yoke seam.

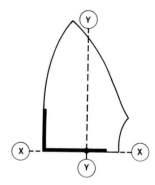

Fig. 18.38.

Stage 2: Remain on Y axis (Fig. 18.39).
- Align origin point to G.
- Mark part of yoke seam.
- Mark armhole seam nip.

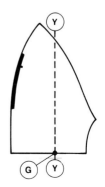

Fig. 18.39.

Stage 3: Remain on Y axis (Fig. 18.40).
- Align origin point to E.
- Complete yoke line.
- Mark end of overarm seam.

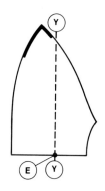

Fig. 18.40.

Stage 4: Align X axes of pattern and paper (Fig. 18.41).
- Align Y axis of pattern to $\frac{L}{2}$ axis on paper.

- Complete CB.
- Mark start of neckline.

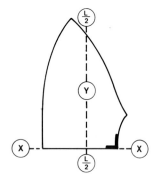

Fig. 18.41.

Stage 5: Remain $\frac{L}{2}$ axis (Fig. 18.42).
- Align origin point to F.
- Complete neck line.
- Mark start of shoulder line.

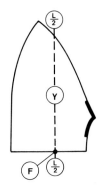

Fig. 18.42.

Stage 6: Remain on $\dfrac{L}{2}$ axis (Fig. 18.43).

- Align origin point to G.
- Complete shoulder line.
- Mark shoulder nip.
- Mark part of overarm seam.

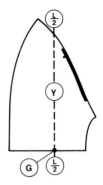

Fig. 18.43.

Stage 7: Use pattern to blend the line of the sleeve cap section (Fig. 18.44).

Fig. 18.44.

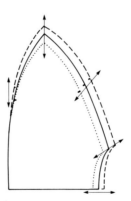

Fig. 18.45. Grade for back yoke.

Grading instructions:
ANORAK SLEEVE

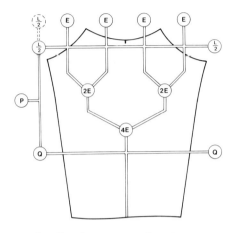

Fig. 18.46. Grading increments for sleeve.

Interval	E	L	$\frac{L}{2}$	P	Q
			Increment values		
4 cm	2.5	5	2.5	10	5
5 cm	3	6	3	12	6

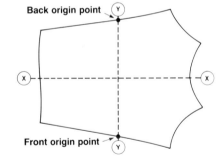

Fig. 18.47. Grading axes.

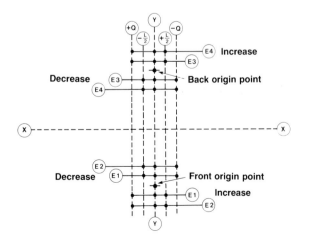

Fig. 18.48. Increment net.

Stage 1: Align Y axes of pattern and paper
(Fig. 18.49).
- Align front origin point to E1.
- Mark part of front sleeve seam.

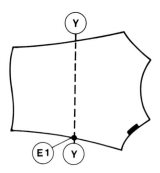

Fig. 18.49.

Stage 2: Remain on Y axis (Fig. 18.50).
- Align front origin point to E2.
- Mark end of sleeve seam and start of underarm
  seam.

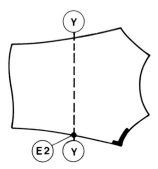

Fig. 18.50.

Stage 3: Remain on Y axis (Fig. 18.51).
- Align back origin point to E3.
- Mark part of back sleeve seam.

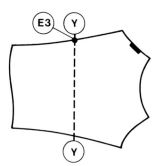

Fig. 18.51.

Stage 4: Remain on Y axis (Fig. 18.52).
● Align back origin point to E4.
● Mark end of sleeve seam and start of underarm seam.

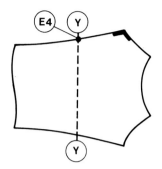

Fig. 18.52.

Stage 5: Align Y axis of pattern to Q axis on paper (Fig. 18.53).
● Align front origin point to E2.
● Mark end of underarm seam and part of cuff.

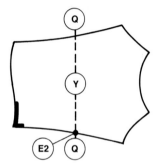

Fig. 18.53.

Stage 6: Remain on Q axis (Fig. 18.54).
● Align X axes of pattern and paper.
● Mark central section of cuff.

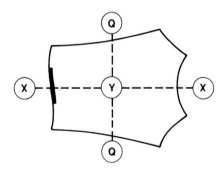

Fig. 18.54.

Stage 7: Remain on Q axis (Fig. 18.55).
- Align back origin point to E4.
- Mark end of underarm seam.
- Complete cuff.

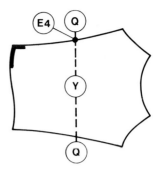

Fig. 18.55.

Stage 8: Align Y axis of pattern to $\frac{L}{2}$ axis on paper

(Fig. 18.56).
- Align front origin point to E1.
- Mark start of sleeve seam.
- Mark start of yoke seam.

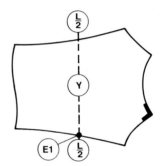

Fig. 18.56.

Stage 9: Remain on $\frac{L}{2}$ axis (Fig. 18.57).

- Align X axes of pattern and paper.
- Mark central section of yoke seam.
- Mark overarm seam nip.

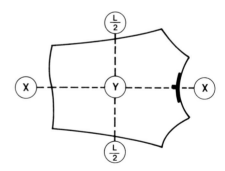

Fig. 18.57.

Stage 10: Remain on $\frac{L}{2}$ axis (Fig. 18.58).

- Align back origin point to E3.
- Mark start of sleeve seam.
- Mark start of yoke seam.

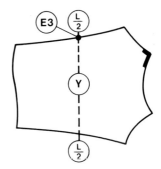

Fig. 18.58.

Stage 11: Use pattern to (Fig. 18.59):
- Blend sleeve seams.
- Complete underarm seams.

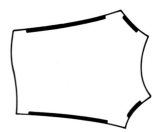

Fig. 18.59.

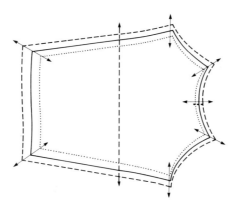

Fig. 18.60. Grade for sleeve.

Grading instructions: ANORAK HOOD

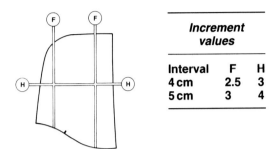

Increment values		
Interval	F	H
4 cm	2.5	3
5 cm	3	4

Fig. 18.61. Grading increments for attached hood.

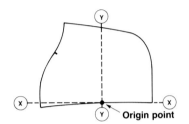

Fig. 18.62. Grading axes.

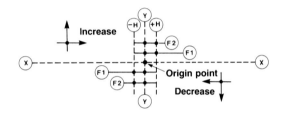

Fig. 18.63. Increment net.

Stage 1: Align X and Y axes of pattern and paper (Fig. 18.64).
● Mark lower section of front edge.
● Mark start of neck line.

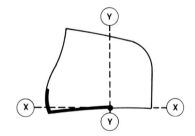

Fig. 18.64.

Stage 2: Remain on Y axis (Fig. 18.65).
● Align origin point to F1.
● Mark central section of neck line.
● Mark shoulder seam nip.

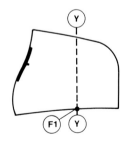

Fig. 18.65.

Stage 3: Remain on Y axis (Fig. 18.66).
- Align origin point to F2.
- Complete neck line.
- Mark start of back seam.

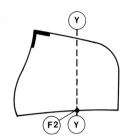

Fig. 18.66.

Stage 4: Align X axes of pattern and paper (Fig. 18.67).
- Align Y axis of pattern to H axis on paper.
- Complete front edge.
- Mark part of crown seam.

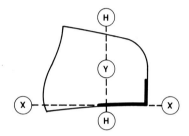

Fig. 18.67.

Stage 5: Remain on H axis (Fig. 18.68).
- Align origin point to F2.
- Mark rounded section of crown seam.

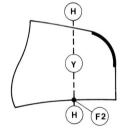

Fig. 18.68.

Stage 6: Use pattern to complete the back section of the crown seam (Fig. 18.69).

Fig. 18.69.

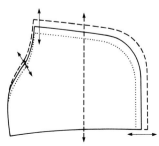

Fig. 18.70. Grade for hood.

Chapter 19

Blouson with One-Piece Raglan Sleeve

This is a mid-hip length garment and the body section can be gauged or pleated on to the waist band. There is a strap front, an all round body seam and a vertical seam on the front for the pocket opening. The body grade follows the lines of the basic grade for body garments and two new grading procedures are introduced and demonstrated:

(1)   The grade of a one-piece full raglan sleeve.

(2)   The grade for a patrol collar, which is sometimes called a mandarin collar.

The sleeve grade shown is for a deepened armhole but the same principles would apply for a regular depth armhole.

All the components are numbered and the demonstrations follow the numerical sequence given in Fig. 19.2.

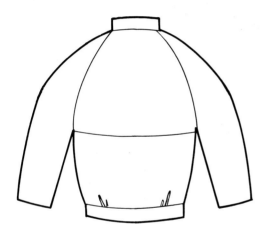

Fig. 19.1. Blouson with one-piece raglan sleeve.

Grading instructions:
BLOUSON FRONT – PART 1

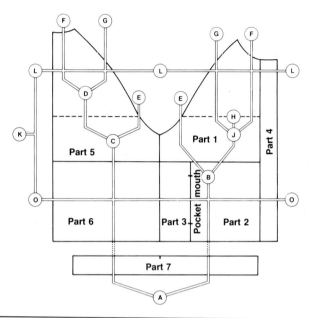

Interval	A	B	C	D	E	F	G	H	J	K	L	O
4 cm	20	12.5	7.5	5	2.5	2.5	2.5	5	10	10	5	5
5 cm	25	16	9	6	3	3	3	7	13	12	6	6

Increment values

Fig. 19.2. Grading increments for body.

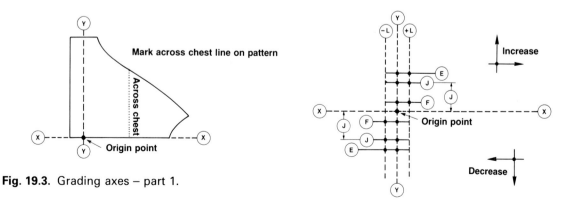

Fig. 19.3. Grading axes – part 1.

Fig. 19.4. Increment net – part 1.

Stage 1: Align X and Y axes of pattern and paper (Fig. 19.5).
- Mark part of front seam.
- Mark part of body seam.

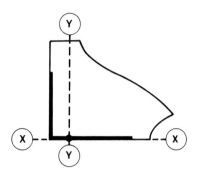

Fig. 19.5.

Stage 2: Remain on Y axis (Fig. 19.6).
- Align origin point to J.
- Mark lower section of armhole from across chest line down.

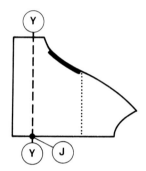

Fig. 19.6.

Stage 3: Remain on Y axis (Fig. 19.7).
- Align origin point to E.
- Complete lower section of armhole.
- Mark side seam and complete body seam.

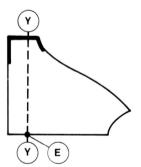

Fig. 19.7.

207

Stage 4: Align X axes of pattern and paper
(Fig. 19.8).
- Align Y axis of pattern to L axis on paper.
- Complete front seam.
- Mark start of neck line.

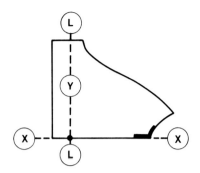

Fig. 19.8.

Stage 5: Remain on L axis (Fig. 19.9).
- Align origin point to F.
- Complete neck line.
- Mark start of armhole seam.

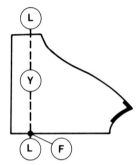

Fig. 19.9.

Stage 6: Use pattern to complete the armhole seam
(Fig. 19.10).

The finished grade for this part is shown in Fig. 19.28.

Fig. 19.10.

Grading instructions:
BLOUSON FRONT – PART 2

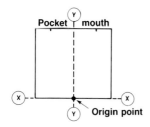

Fig. 19.11. Grading axes – part 2.

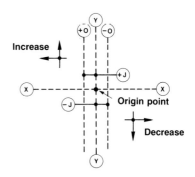

Fig. 19.12. Increment net – part 2.

Stage 1: Align X and Y axes of pattern and paper (Fig. 19.13).
- Mark part of front seam.
- Mark part of body seam.

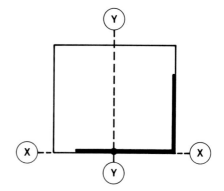

Fig. 19.13.

Stage 2: Remain on Y axis (Fig. 19.14).
- Align origin point to J.
- Complete body seam.
- Mark part of pocket seam and nips.

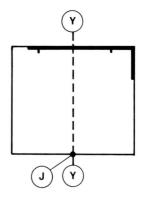

Fig. 19.14.

Stage 3: Align X axes of pattern and paper
(Fig. 19.15).
- Align Y axis of pattern to O axis on paper.
- Complete front seam.
- Mark part of waist seam.

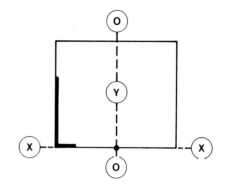

Fig. 19.15.

Stage 4: Remain aligned to O axis (Fig. 19.16).
- Move pattern along O axis until pocket seam aligns
  with the line drawn in Stage 2.
- Complete pocket seam.
- Complete waist seam.

The finished grade for this part is shown in Fig. 19.28.

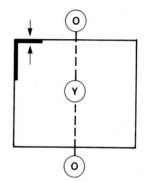

Fig. 19.16.

Grading instructions:
BLOUSON FRONT – PART 3

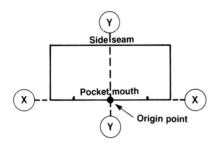

Fig. 19.17. Grading axes – part 3.

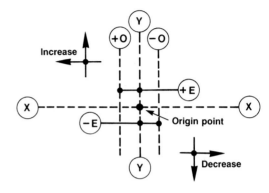

Fig. 19.18. Increment net – part 3.

Stage 1: Align X and Y axes of pattern and paper
(Fig. 19.19).
- Mark part of pocket seam and nips.
- Mark part of body seam.

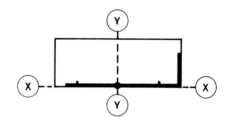

Fig. 19.19.

Stage 2: Remain on Y axis (Fig. 19.20).
- Align origin point to E.
- Complete body seam.
- Mark part of side seam.

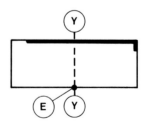

Fig. 19.20.

Stage 3: Align X axes of pattern and paper
(Fig. 19.21).
- Align Y axis of pattern to O axis on paper.
- Complete pocket seam.
- Mark part of waist seam.

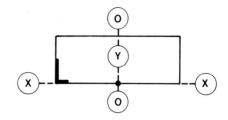

Fig. 19.21.

Stage 4: Remain aligned to O axis (Fig. 19.22).
- Move pattern along O axis until side seam aligns
  with the line marked in Stage 2.
- Complete side seam.
- Complete waist seam.

The finished grade for this part is shown in Fig. 19.28.

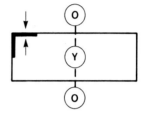

Fig. 19.22.

Grading instructions:
BLOUSON FRONT – PART 4

Fig. 19.23. Grading axes – part 4.

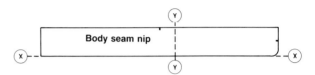

Fig. 19.24. Increment net – part 4.

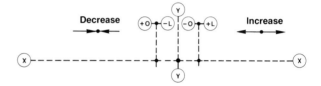

Stage 1: Align X and Y axes of pattern and paper (Fig. 19.25).
- Mark part of front edge.
- Mark part of front seam.
- Mark body seam nip.

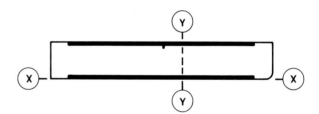

Fig. 19.25.

Stage 2: Remain aligned to X axis (Fig. 19.26).
- Align Y axis of pattern to L axis on paper.
- Complete top end of strap.
- Mark CF nip.

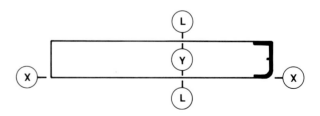

Fig. 19.26.

Stage 3: Remain aligned to X axis (Fig. 19.27).
● Align Y axis of pattern to O axis on paper.
● Complete lower end of strap.

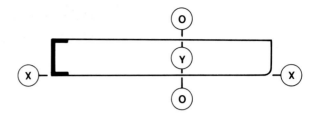

Fig. 19.27.

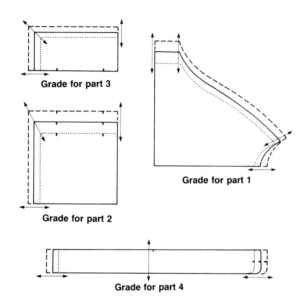

Grade for part 3

Grade for part 2

Grade for part 1

Grade for part 4

Fig. 19.28. Total grade for front.

Grading instructions:
BLOUSON BACK – PART 5

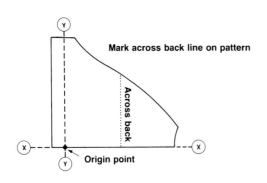

Fig. **19.29**. Grading axes – part 5.

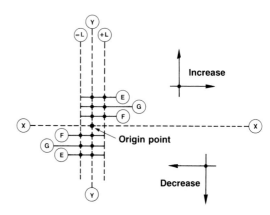

Fig. **19.30**. Increment net – part 5.

Stage 1: Align X and Y axes of pattern and paper (Fig. 19.31).
- Mark part of CB.
- Mark part of body seam.

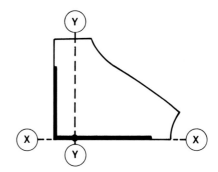

Fig. **19.31**.

Stage 2: Remain on Y axis (Fig. 19.32).
- Align origin point to G.
- Mark lower section of armhole from across back line down.

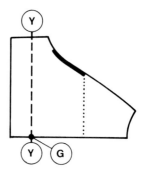

Fig. **19.32**.

Stage 3: Remain on Y axis (Fig. 19.33).
- Align origin point to E.
- Complete lower section of armhole.
- Mark side seam.
- Complete body seam.

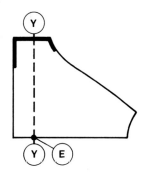

Fig. 19.33.

Stage 4: Align X axes of pattern and paper (Fig. 19.34).
- Align Y axis of pattern to L axis on paper.
- Complete CB.
- Mark start of neck line.

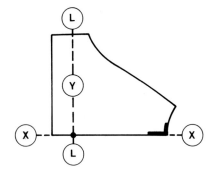

Fig. 19.34.

Stage 5: Remain aligned to L axis (Fig. 19.35).
- Align origin point to F.
- Complete neck line.
- Mark start of armhole seam.

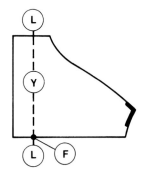

Fig. 19.35.

Stage 6: Use pattern to complete the armhole seam (Fig. 19.36).

The completed grade for this part is shown in Fig. 19.48.

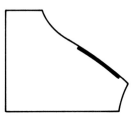

Fig. 19.36.

Grading instructions:
BLOUSON BACK – PART 6

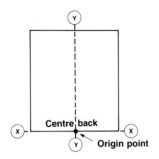

Fig. 19.37. Grading axes – part 6.

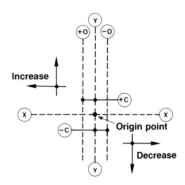

Fig. 19.38. Increment net – part 6.

Stage 1: Align X and Y axes of pattern and paper (Fig. 19.39).
- Mark part of CB.
- Mark part of body seam.

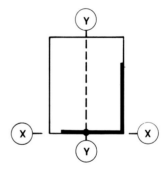

Fig. 19.39.

Stage 2: Remain on Y axis (Fig. 19.40).
- Align origin point to C.
- Complete body seam.
- Mark part of side seam.

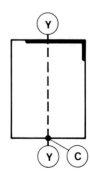

Fig. 19.40.

Stage 3: Align X axis of pattern and paper
(Fig. 19.41).
- Align Y axis of pattern to O axis on paper.
- Complete CB.
- Mark part of waist seam.

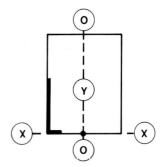

Fig. 19.41.

Stage 4: Remain on O axis (Fig. 19.42).
- Move pattern along O axis until the side seam
  aligns with the section marked in Stage 2.
- Complete side seam and waist seam.

The finished grade for this part is shown in Fig. 19.48.

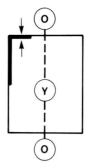

Fig. 19.42.

Grading instructions:
BLOUSON BAND – PART 7

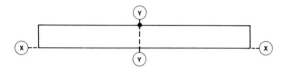

Fig. 19.43. Grading axes – part 7.

Fig. 19.44. Increment net – part 7.

Stage 1: Align X and Y axes of pattern and paper (Fig. 19.45).
- Mark part of waist seam and hem line.

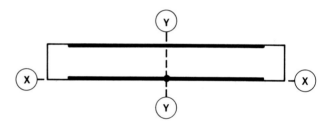

Fig. 19.45.

Stage 2: Remain on X axis (Fig. 19.46).
- Align Y axis of pattern to B axis on paper.
- Complete front section of band.

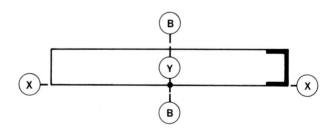

Fig. 19.46.

Stage 3: Remain on X axis (Fig. 19.47).
- Align Y axis of pattern to C axis on paper.
- Complete CB section of band.

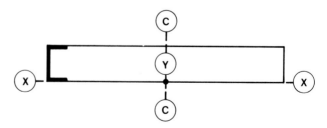

Fig. 19.47.

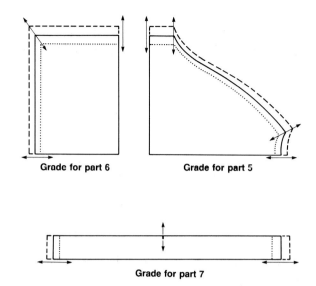

Fig. 19.48. Total grade for back.

Grading instructions:
BLOUSON SLEEVE

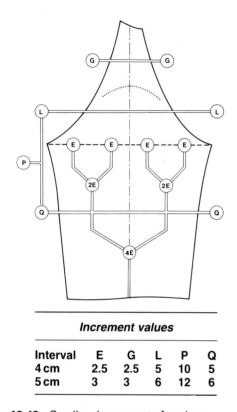

Increment values

Interval	E	G	L	P	Q
4 cm	2.5	2.5	5	10	5
5 cm	3	3	6	12	6

Fig. 19.49. Grading increments for sleeve.

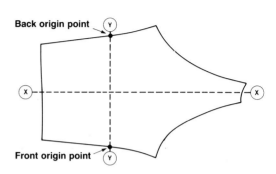

Fig. 19.50. Grading axes.

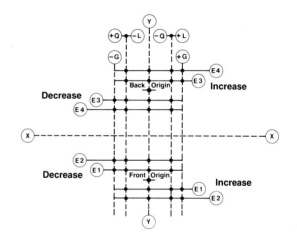

Fig. 19.51. Increment net.

Stage 1: Align Y axes of pattern and paper (Fig. 19.52).
- Align front origin point to E1.
- Mark lower part of sleeve seam.

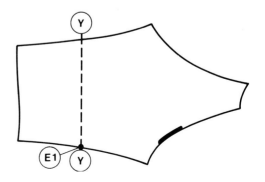

Fig. 19.52.

Stage 2:   Remain on Y axis (Fig. 19.53).
- Align front origin point to E2.
- Complete lower part of sleeve seam.
- Mark start of underarm seam.

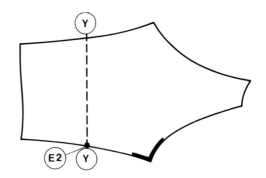

Fig. 19.53.

Stage 3:   Align Y axis on pattern to Q axis on paper (Fig. 19.54).
- Align front origin point to E2.
- Mark lower part of sleeve seam and part of cuff.

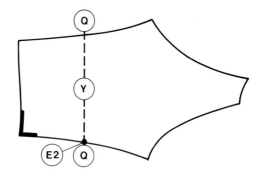

Fig. 19.54.

Stage 4:   Remain on Q axis (Fig. 19.55).
- Align X axes of pattern and paper.
- Mark central section of cuff.

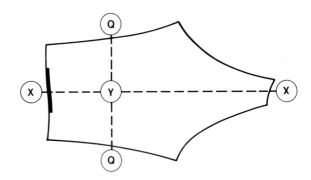

Fig. 19.55.

Stage 5:   Remain on Q axis (Fig. 19.56).
- Align back origin point to E4.
- Mark part of cuff.
- Mark end of underarm seam.

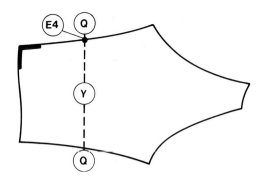

Fig. 19.56.

Stage 6:   Align Y axes of pattern and paper (Fig. 19.57).
- Align back origin point to E3.
- Mark lower part of sleeve seam.

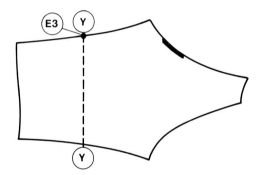

Fig. 19.57.

Stage 7:   Remain on Y axis (Fig. 19.58).
- Align back origin point to E4.
- Complete lower part of sleeve seam.
- Mark start of underseam.

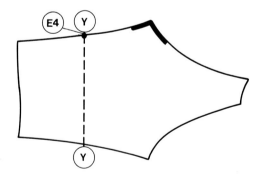

Fig. 19.58.

Stage 8: Align X axes of pattern and paper
(Fig. 19.59).
- Align Y axis of pattern to L axis on paper.
- Mark a small section of the back and front sleeve
  seams.

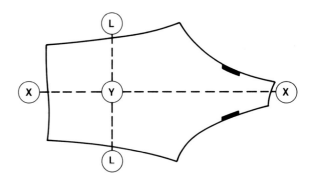

Fig. 19.59.

Stage 9: Remain on X axis (Fig. 19.60).
- Align Y axis of pattern to G axis on paper.
- Mark neck line and start of sleeve horn seams.

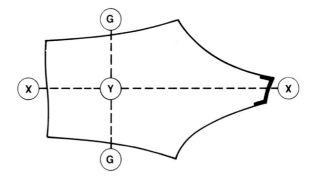

Fig. 19.60.

Stage 10: Use pattern to (Fig. 19.61).
- Complete underarm seams.
- Blend sleeve seams.

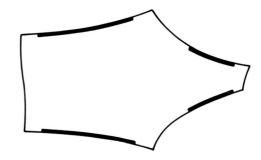

Fig. 19.61.

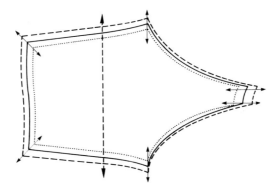

Fig. 19.62. Grade for sleeve.

Grading instructions:
BLOUSON COLLAR

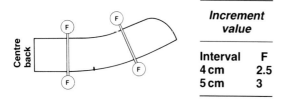

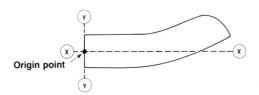

Increment value	
Interval	**F**
4 cm	2.5
5 cm	3

Fig. 19.63. Grading increments for collar.

Fig. 19.64. Grading axes.

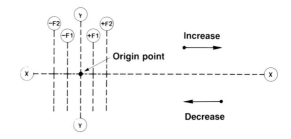

Fig. 19.65. Increment net.

Stage 1: Align X and Y axes of pattern and paper (Fig. 19.66).
- Mark CB section of collar.

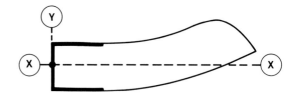

Fig. 19.66.

Stage 2: Remain on X axis (Fig. 19.67).
- Align origin point to F1.
- Mark central section of collar.
- Mark shoulder nip.

Fig. 19.67.

Stage 3:   Remain on X axis (Fig. 19.68).
- Align origin point to F2.
- Complete collar.

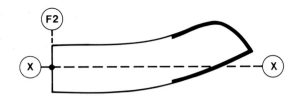

Fig. 19.68.

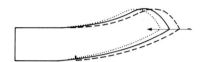

Fig. 19.69.

Chapter 20

Bathrobe with Kimono Sleeve

This is a wrap-type, knee length coat with a tie belt and a three-quarter length kimono sleeve. The rounded side vents are open from mid-thigh and the shawl collar is cut in one piece with the front.

The features of this demonstration are the grades for the:

- Kimono sleeve.
- Shawl collar and facing.

- A proportionate grade for the patch pocket.
- Side vent facings.

The back and front grades both have two stages of grading – the body and then the sleeve – with each stage derived from the basic grades for these two parts.

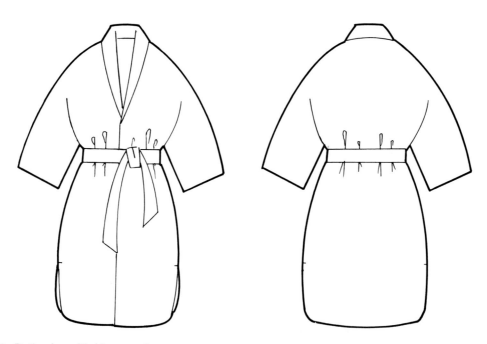

Fig. 20.1. Bathrobe with kimono sleeve.

Grading instructions:
BATHROBE FRONT

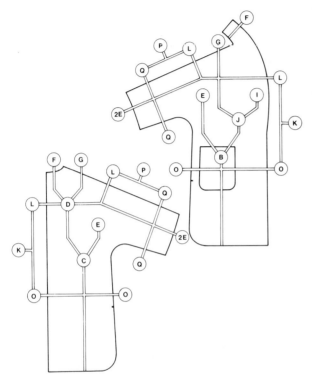

	Increment values						
Interval	B	C	D	E	2E	F	G
4 cm	12.5	7.5	5	2.5	5	2.5	2.5
5 cm	16	9	6	3	6	3	3
Interval	I	J	K	L	O	P	Q
4 cm	7.5	10	15	5	10	10	5
5 cm	10	13	18	6	12	12	6

Fig. 20.2. Grading increments for body and sleeve.

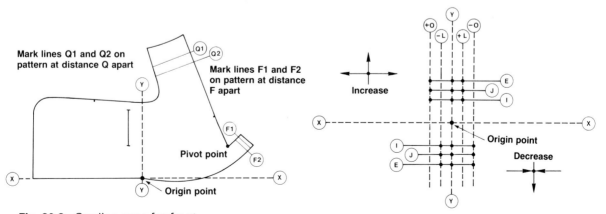

Mark lines Q1 and Q2 on pattern at distance Q apart

Mark lines F1 and F2 on pattern at distance F apart

Pivot point

Origin point

Fig. 20.3. Grading axes for front.

Increase

Decrease

Origin point

Fig. 20.4. Increment net.

Stage 1: Align X and Y axes of pattern and paper (Fig. 20.5).
- Mark part of front edge and start of lapel section.

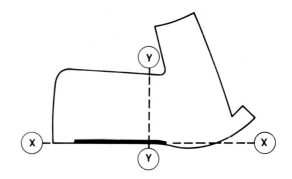

Fig. 20.5.

Stage 2: Remain on Y axis (Fig. 20.6).
- Align origin point to I.
- Mark front top-corner of pocket.

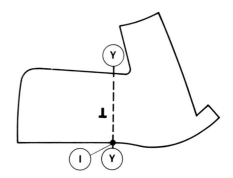

Fig. 20.6.

Stage 3: Remain on Y axis (Fig. 20.7).
- Align origin point to J.
- Mark back top-corner of pocket.

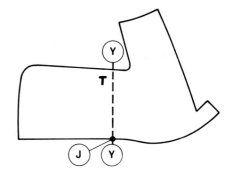

Fig. 20.7.

Stage 4: Remain on Y axis (Fig. 20.8).
- Align origin point to E.
- Mark part of side seam and underarm seam.
- **To increase:** Mark Q1 line on paper.
- **To decrease:** Mark Q2 line on paper.

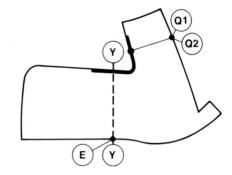

Fig. 20.8.

Stage 5: Align X and Y axes of pattern and paper (Fig. 20.9).
- Align Y axis of pattern to O axis on paper.
- Complete lower section of front edge.
- Mark part of hem.

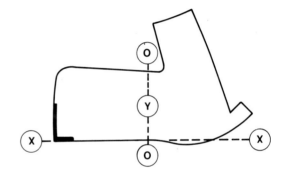

Fig. 20.9.

Stage 6: Remain aligned to O axis (Fig. 20.10).
- Move pattern along O axis until the side seam touches the section marked in stage 4.
- Complete side seam and hem.
- Mark vent nip.

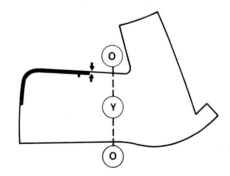

Fig. 20.10.

Stage 7A: **To increase** (Fig. 20.11):
- Move underseam of pattern along the section marked in Stage 4 until Q2 aligns with Q1.
- Mark end of sleeve and part of cuff.
- Mark intersection of overarm seam and the aligned Q lines.

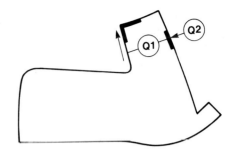

Fig. 20.11.

Stage 7B: **To decrease** (Fig. 20.12):
- Move underseam of pattern along the section marked in Stage 4 until Q1 aligns with Q2.
- Mark end of sleeve and part of cuff.
- Mark intersection of overarm seam and the aligned Q lines.

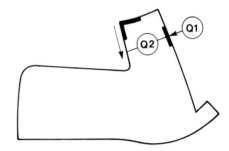

Fig. 20.12.

Stage 8: Mark the value of increment 2E from the intersection point marked in the previous stage (Fig. 20.13).
- **To increase**: Mark above intersection point.
- **To decrease**: Mark below intersection point.

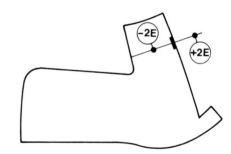

Fig. 20.13.

Stage 9A: **To increase** (Fig. 20.14):
- Align Q2 on pattern to Q1 on paper (as stage 7A).
- Move Q2 along Q1 until overarm seam aligns with increment 2E.
- Complete cuff and mark end of overarm seam.

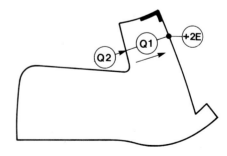

Fig. 20.14.

Stage 9B: **To decrease** (Fig. 20.15):
- Align Q1 on pattern to Q2 on paper (as stage 7B).
- Move Q1 along Q2 until overarm seam aligns with increment 2E.
- Complete cuff and mark end of overarm seam.

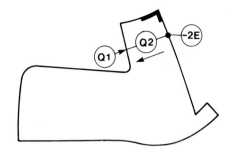

Fig. 20.15.

Stage 10: Align Y axis of pattern to L axis on paper (Fig. 20.16).
- Align origin point to I.
- Mark pivot point at front neck point.
- Mark start of shoulder line.

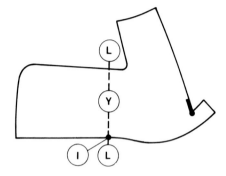

Fig. 20.16.

Stage 11: Remain on L axis (Fig. 20.17).
- Align origin point to J.
- Complete shoulder line and extend over the shoulder point curve.
- Mark shoulder nip.

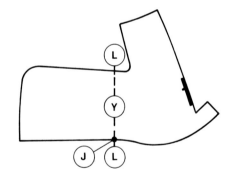

Fig. 20.17.

Stage 12: Use an awl to align the pivot point of the pattern to the pivot point on the paper (stage 10) (Fig. 20.18).
- Pivot from this point until the lower part of the lapel section aligns with the line marked in Stage 1.
- Mark lapel and collar line.
- Mark neck seam of CB section.
- **To increase**: Mark line F1 on paper.
- **To decrease**: Mark line F2 on paper.

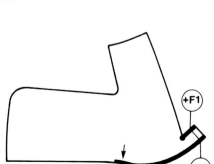

Fig. 20.18.

Stage 13A: **To increase** (Fig. 20.19):
- Move pattern along the marked neck seam until F2 aligns with F1.
- Complete CB section of collar.

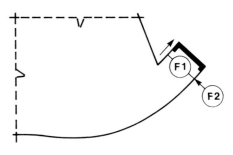

Fig. 20.19.

Stage 13B: **To decrease** (Fig. 20.20):
- Move pattern along the marked neck seam until F1 aligns with F2.
- Complete CB section of collar.

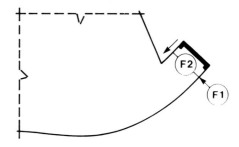

Fig. 20.20.

Stage 14:   Use the pattern to complete the overarm seam from the shoulder section to the cuff (Fig. 20.21). The difference between the pattern length and that marked will be equal to the total sleeve length grade of increment P.

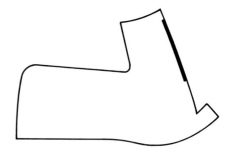

Fig. 20.21.

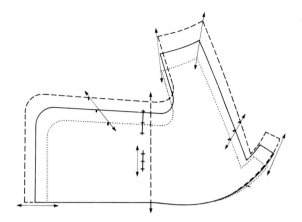

Fig. 20.22. Grade for front and sleeve.

Grading instructions:
BATHROBE BACK

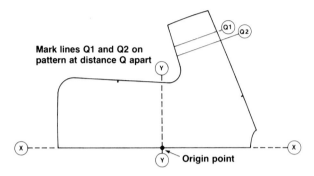

Fig. 20.23. Grading axes for back.

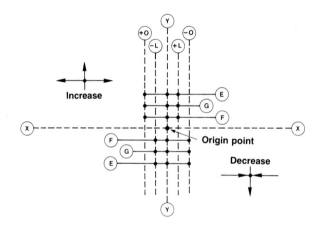

Fig. 20.24. Increment net.

Stage 1: Align X and Y axes of pattern and paper
(Fig. 20.25).
- Mark part of CB.

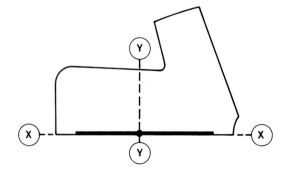

Fig. 20.25.

Stage 2: Remain on Y axis (Fig. 20.26).
- Align origin point to E.
- Mark part of side seam and underarm seam.
- **To increase**: Mark Q1 line on paper.
- **To decrease**: Mark Q2 line on paper.

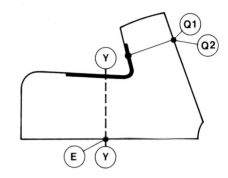

Fig. 20.26.

Stage 3: Align X axes of pattern and paper (Fig. 20.27).
- Align Y axis of pattern to O axis on paper.
- Complete lower section of CB.
- Mark part of hem.

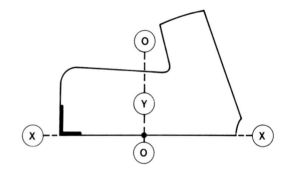

Fig. 20.27.

Stage 4: Remain aligned to O axis (Fig. 20.28).
- Move pattern along O axis until the side seam touches the section marked in stage 2.
- Complete side seam and hem.
- Mark vent nip.

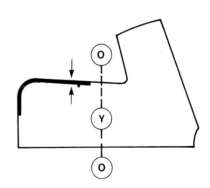

Fig. 20.28.

Stage 5: Align X axes of pattern and paper (Fig. 20.29).
- Align Y axis of pattern to L axis on paper.
- Complete CB and mark start of neck line.

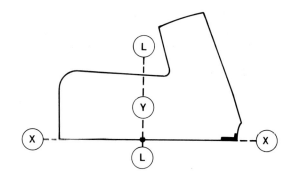

Fig. 20.29.

Stage 6: Remain on L axis (Fig. 20.30).
- Align origin point to F.
- Complete neck line and mark start of shoulder.

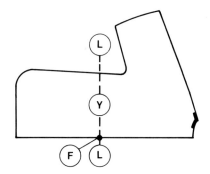

Fig. 20.30.

Stage 7: Remain on L axis (Fig. 20.31).
- Align origin point to G.
- Complete shoulder line and extend over the shoulder point curve.
- Mark shoulder nip.

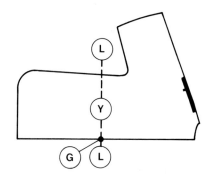

Fig. 20.31.

Stage 8A: **To increase** (Fig. 20.32).
- Move underseam of pattern along the section marked in Stage 2 until Q2 aligns with Q1.
- Mark end of sleeve and part of cuff.
- Mark intersection of overarm seam and the aligned Q lines.

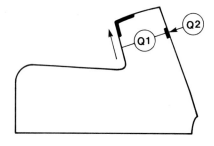

Fig. 20.32.

Stage 8B: **To decrease** (Fig. 20.33):
- Move underseam of pattern along the section marked in Stage 2 until Q1 aligns with Q2.
- Mark end of sleeve and part of cuff.
- Mark intersection of overarm seam and the aligned Q lines.

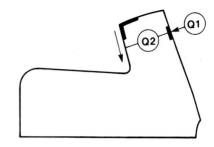

Fig. 20.33.

Stage 9: Mark the value of increment 2E from the intersection point marked in the previous stage (Fig. 20.34).
- **To increase**: Mark above intersection point.
- **To decrease**: Mark below intersection point.

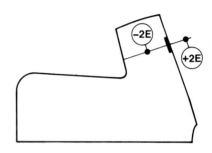

Fig. 20.34.

Stage 10A: **To increase** (Fig. 20.35):
- Align Q2 on pattern to Q1 on paper (as stage 2).
- Move Q2 along Q1 until overarm seam aligns with increment 2E.
- Complete cuff and mark end of overarm seam.

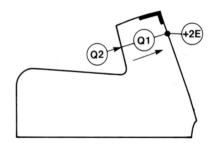

Fig. 20.35.

Stage 10B: **To decrease** (Fig. 20.36):
- Align Q1 on pattern to Q2 on paper (as stage 2).
- Move Q1 along Q2 until overarm seam aligns with 2E.
- Complete cuff and mark end of overarm seam.

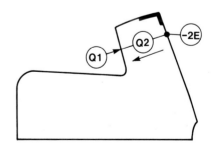

Fig. 20.36.

Stage 11: Use pattern to complete the overarm seam from the shoulder section to the cuff (Fig. 20.37). The difference between the pattern length and that marked will be equal to the total sleeve length grade of increment P.

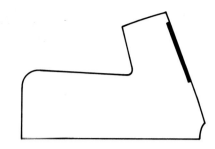

Fig. 20.37.

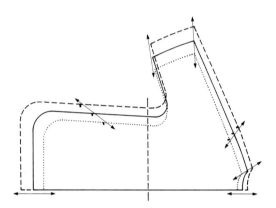

Fig. 20.38. Grade for back and sleeve.

Grading instructions:
SHAWL COLLAR FACING

Mark lines F1 and F2 on
pattern at distance F apart

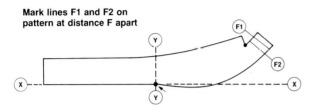

Fig. 20.39. Grading axes for facing.

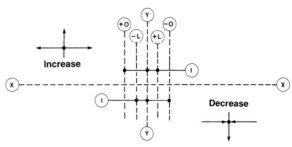

Fig. 20.40. Increment net.

Stage 1: Align X and Y axes of pattern (Fig. 20.41).
- Mark part of front edge and start of lapel.
- Mark part of inside edge.

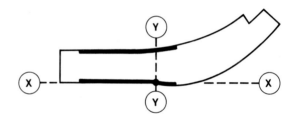

Fig. 20.41.

Stage 2: Remain aligned to X axis
(Fig. 20.42).
- Align Y axis of pattern to O axis on paper.
- Complete lower section of facing.

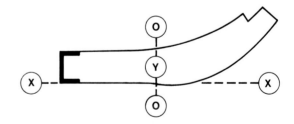

Fig. 20.42.

Stage 3: Align Y axis of pattern to L axis on paper
(Fig. 20.43).
- Align origin point to I.
- Mark pivot point.
- Mark shoulder section of facing.

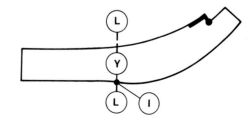

Fig. 20.43.

Stage 4: Use an awl to align the pivot point of the pattern to the pivot point marked in the previous stage (Fig. 20.44).
- Pivot from this point until the lower part of the lapel section aligns with the line marked in Stage 1.
- Mark lapel and collar line.
- Mark neck seam of the CB section.
- **To increase**: Mark line F1 on paper.
- **To decrease**: Mark line F2 on paper.

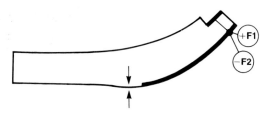

Fig. 20.44.

Stage 5A: **To increase** (Fig. 20.45):
- Move pattern along the marked neck seam until F2 aligns with F1.
- Complete CB section of collar.

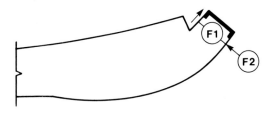

Fig. 20.45.

Stage 5B: **To decrease** (Fig. 20.46):
- Move pattern along the marked neck seam until F1 aligns with F2.
- Complete CB section of collar.

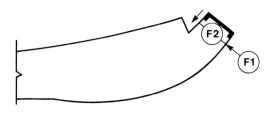

Fig. 20.46.

Stage 6: Use pattern to complete the inside edge from the shoulder section down to the line marked in Stage 1 (Fig. 20.47).

Fig. 20.47.

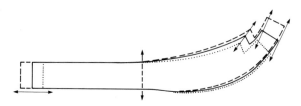

Fig. 20.48. Grade for facing.

Grading instructions:
PATCH POCKET

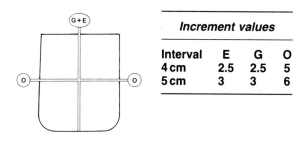

Fig. 20.49. Grading increments for patch pocket.

Increment values			
Interval	E	G	O
4 cm	2.5	2.5	5
5 cm	3	3	6

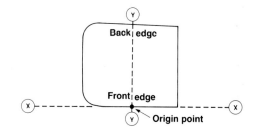

Fig. 20.50. Grading axes.

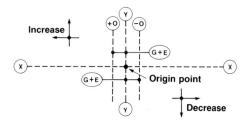

Fig. 20.51. Increment net.

Stage 1: Align X and Y axes of pattern and paper (Fig. 20.52).

● Mark part of front edge and pocket mouth.

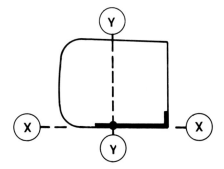

Fig. 20.52.

Stage 2:   Remain on Y axis (Fig. 20.53).
- Align origin point to E + G.
- Mark part of back edge and pocket mouth.

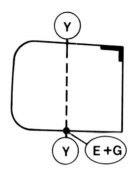

Fig. 20.53.

Stage 3:   Remain aligned to E + G (Fig. 20.54).
- Align Y axis of pattern to O axis on paper.
- Mark lower part of back edge.
- Mark back corner and part of lower edge.

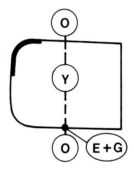

Fig. 20.54.

Stage 4:   Remain aligned to O axis (Fig. 20.55).
- Align origin point to X axis.
- Complete front edge and corner.
- Complete lower edge.

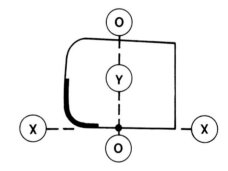

Fig. 20.55.

Stage 5:   Use pattern to (Fig. 20.56).
- Complete pocket mouth.
- Complete back edge.

Fig. 20.56.

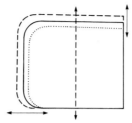

Fig. 20.57. Grade for patch pocket.

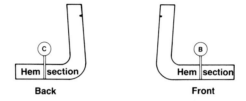

Back   **Front**

Fig. 20.58. Grading increments for side vent facings.

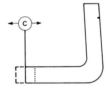

**Increase or decrease length of hem section
by selected value of increment C**

Fig. 20.59. Grade for back facing.

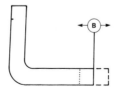

**Increase or decrease length of hem section
by selected value of increment B**

Fig. 20.60. Grade for front facing.

Chapter 21

Pyjama Trouser

A cut very often used for pyjama trousers is that in which the conventional side seam is eliminated and the back and front panels are combined into one piece. This grade is derived from the basic trouser grade but the secondary girth grades of the knee and bottom are ignored. As the waist and girth size intervals are the same, increment A serves for both these grades.

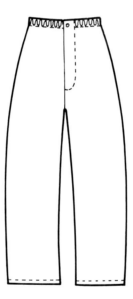

Fig. 21.1. Pyjama trouser.

Grading instructions:
PYJAMA TROUSER

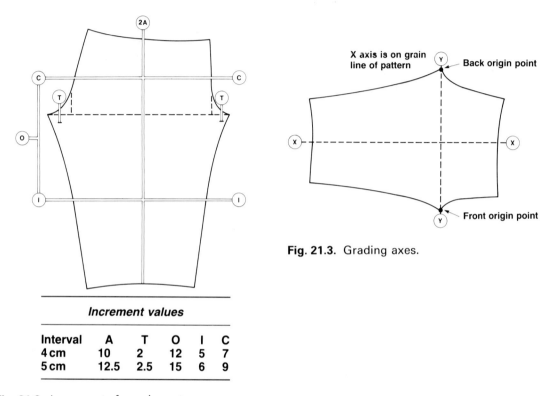

Fig. 21.3. Grading axes.

Increment values

Interval	A	T	O	I	C
4 cm	10	2	12	5	7
5 cm	12.5	2.5	15	6	9

Fig. 21.2. Increments for pyjama trouser.

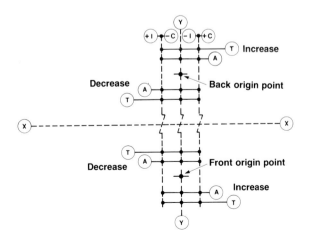

Fig. 21.4. Increment net.

Stage 1:   Align Y axes of pattern and paper (Fig. 21.5).
- Align front origin point to A.
- Mark part of fly seam.

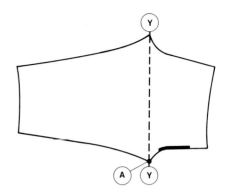

Fig. 21.5.

Stage 2:   Remain on Y axis (Fig. 21.6).
- Align front origin point to T.
- Mark fly seam to crotch point.
- Mark start of inside leg seam.

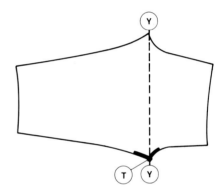

Fig. 21.6.

Stage 3:   Align Y axis of pattern to I axis on paper (Fig. 21.7).
- Align front origin point to A.
- Mark end of inside leg seam.
- Mark part of hem.

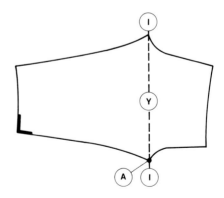

Fig. 21.7.

Stage 4:   Remain on I axis (Fig. 21.8).
● Align X axes of pattern and paper.
● Mark central section of hem.

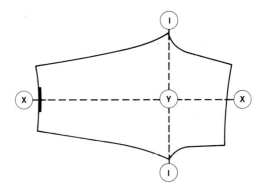

Fig. 21.8.

Stage 5:   Remain on I axis (Fig. 21.9).
● Align back origin point to A.
● Mark end of inside leg seam.
● Complete hem.

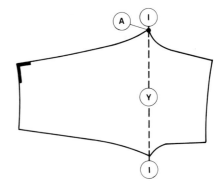

Fig. 21.9.

Stage 6:   Align Y axes of pattern and paper
(Fig. 21.10).
● Align back origin point to A.
● Mark part of seat seam.

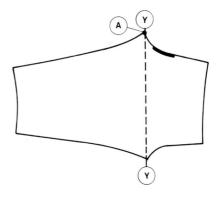

Fig. 21.10.

Stage 7:   Remain on Y axis (Fig. 21.11).
- Align back origin point to T.
- Mark seat seam to crotch point.
- Mark start of inside leg seam.

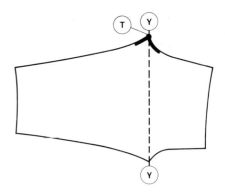

Fig. 21.11.

Stage 8:   Align Y axis of pattern to C axis on paper (Fig. 21.12).
- Align front origin point to A.
- Complete fly seam.
- Mark part of waist line.

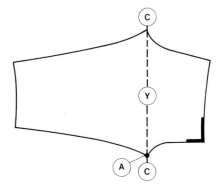

Fig. 21.12.

Stage 9:   Remain on C axis (Fig. 21.13).
- Align X axes of pattern and paper.
- Mark central section of waist line.

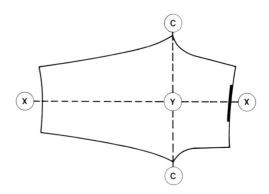

Fig. 21.13.

Stage 10: Remain on C axis (Fig. 21.14).
- Align back origin point to A.
- Complete waist line.
- Complete seat seam.

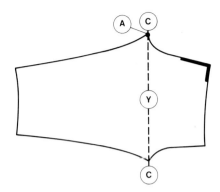

Fig. 21.14.

Stage 11: Use pattern to complete the inside leg seams (Fig. 21.15).

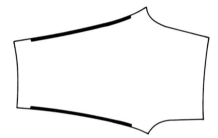

Fig. 21.15.

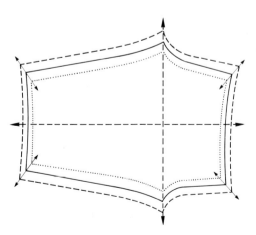

Fig. 21.16. Grade for pyjama trouser.

Chapter 22

T-Shirt

This example demonstrates the application of a traditional sizing system which is widely used throughout the world for underwear, sportswear, pyjamas etc. Instead of a size symbol, each size has a 'name' such as small, medium, large, extra large and so on. The knit fabrics used for underwear have a great deal of extensibility and are cut for comfort in wear, incorporating large ease allowances. Therefore precision sizing is not really necessary.

The size interval itself is based on the equivalent of two sizes, i.e. 8 cm for Continental systems and 10 cm for the British system. Another feature of this demonstration is that it is a 50–50 grade, meaning that the back and front are graded by exactly the same amounts, compared with the regular method which uses different proportions for the back and front sections of the body grade. As the grades for the front and back are exactly the same, only the front grade is demonstrated.

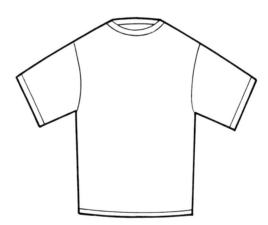

Fig. 22.1. T-shirt.

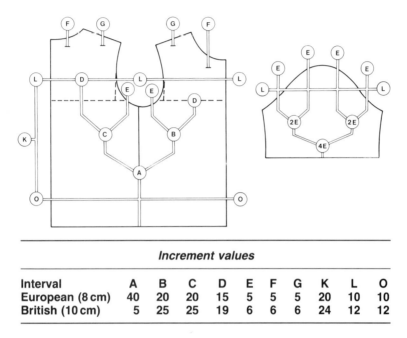

Grading instructions:
T-SHIRT FRONT

Fig. 22.2. Grading increments for T-shirt body and sleeve.

Interval	A	B	C	D	E	F	G	K	L	O
European (8 cm)	40	20	20	15	5	5	5	20	10	10
British (10 cm)	5	25	25	19	6	6	6	24	12	12

Increment values

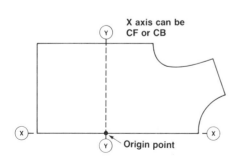

Fig. 22.3. Grading axes for front and back.

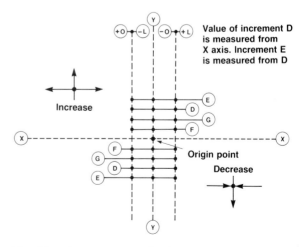

Fig. 22.4. Increment net for front and back.

Stage 1:   Align X and Y axes of pattern and paper
(Fig. 22.5).
- Mark part of CF/CB.

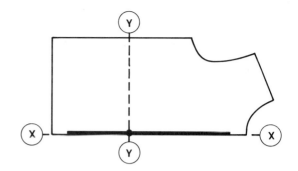

Fig. 22.5.

Stage 2:   Remain on Y axis (Fig. 22.6).
- Align origin point to D.
- Mark part of lower section of armhole.

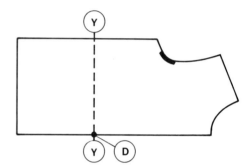

Fig. 22.6.

Stage 3:   Remain on Y axis (Fig. 22.7).
- Align origin point to E.
- Complete lower section of armhole.
- Mark part of side seam.

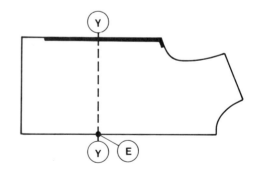

Fig. 22.7.

Stage 4: Align X axes of pattern and paper (Fig. 22.8).
- Align Y axis of pattern to O axis on paper.
- Complete lower section of CF/CB.
- Mark part of hem.

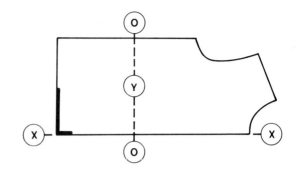

Fig. 22.8.

Stage 5: Remain on O axis (Fig. 22.9).
- Move pattern along O axis until the side seam touches the line marked in Stage 3.
- Complete side seam and hem.

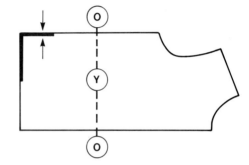

Fig. 22.9.

Stage 6: Align X axes of pattern and paper (Fig. 22.10).
- Align Y axis of pattern to L axis on paper.
- Complete CF/CB.
- Mark start of neck line.

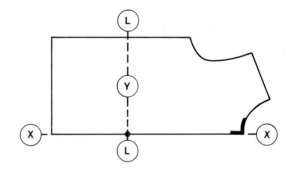

Fig. 22.10.

Stage 7:   Remain on O axis (Fig. 22.11).
- Align origin point to F.
- Complete neck line.
- Mark start of shoulder.

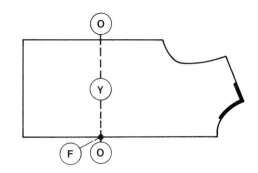

Fig. 22.11.

Stage 8:   Remain on O axis (Fig. 22.12).
- Align origin point to G.
- Complete shoulder line.
- Mark start of armhole.

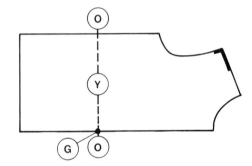

Fig. 22.12.

Stage 9:   Use pattern to blend the armhole line
(Fig. 22.13).

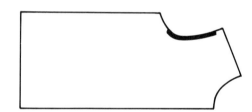

Fig. 22.13.

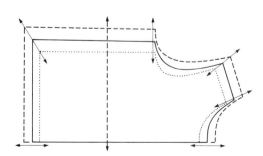

Fig. 22.14. Grade for front.

Grading instructions:
T-SHIRT SLEEVE

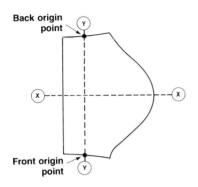

Fig. 22.15. Grading axes for sleeve.

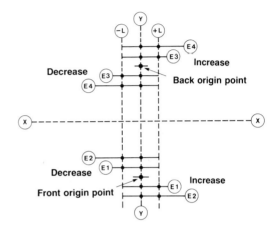

Fig. 22.16. Increment net.

Stage 1: Align Y axes of pattern and paper (Fig. 22.17).
- Align front origin point to E1.
- Mark part of lower section of sleeve head.

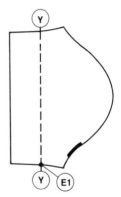

Fig. 22.17.

Stage 2:   Remain on Y axis (Fig. 22.18).
- Align front origin point to E2.
- Complete lower section of sleeve head.
- Mark underarm seam.
- Mark front half of cuff.

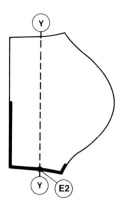

Fig. 22.18.

Stage 3:   Remain on Y axis (Fig. 22.19).
- Align back origin point to E3.
- Mark part of lower section of sleeve head.

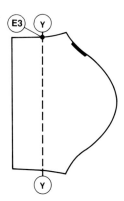

Fig. 22.19.

Stage 4:   Remain on Y axis (Fig. 22.20).
- Align back origin point to E4.
- Complete lower section of sleeve head.
- Mark underarm seam.
- Mark back half of cuff.

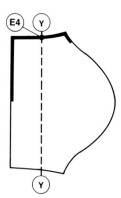

Fig. 22.20.

Stage 5: Align X axes of pattern and paper (Fig. 22.21).
- Align Y axis of pattern to L axis on paper.
- Mark vertex of sleeve head.
- Mark shoulder nip.

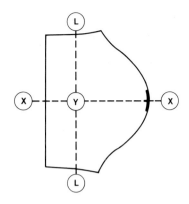

Fig. 22.21.

Stage 6: Use pattern to blend sleeve head run (Fig. 22.22).

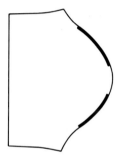

Fig. 22.22.

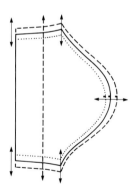

Fig. 22.23. Grade for sleeve.

Chapter 23

Jeans Styled Shorts

The grade of this style demonstrates another and more simple method of grading bifurcated garments when the length of the garment is above the knee. With this method the waist and seat girths are graded in one direction and the completion of the thigh girth grade is effected in the opposite direction.

The hip pocket can be graded proportionately or according to the pre-creasing form sizes available to the factory. If there is a watch-pocket, as with five pocket jeans, then this can be proportionately graded or left the same size for all sizes.

Although the pocket bag usually has a lining join, in this demonstration it is treated as one piece.

Fig. 23.1. Jeans styled shorts.

Grading instructions:
SHORTS – BACK PANEL

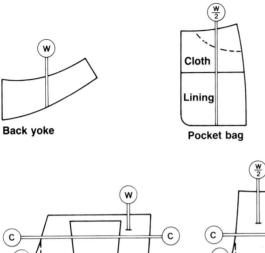

Back yoke

Pocket bag

Increment values						
Interval	W	$\frac{W}{2}$	H	T	C	D
4 cm	10	5	10	2	7	2.5
5 cm	12.5	6.25	12.5	2.5	9	3

Waist and seat girth size intervals are the same

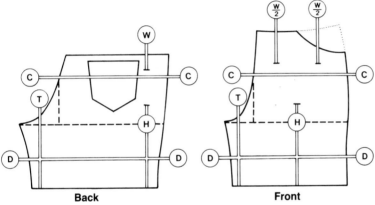

Back

Front

Fig. 23.2. Grading increments for shorts.

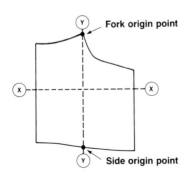

Fig. 23.3. Grading axes for back panel.

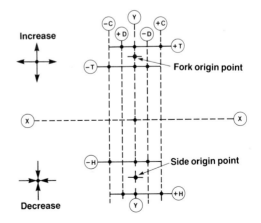

Fig. 23.4. Increment net.

Stage 1:   Align X and Y axes of pattern and paper (Fig. 23.5).
- Mark part of lower section of seat seam.

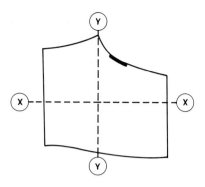

Fig. 23.5.

Stage 2:   Remain on Y axis (Fig. 23.6).
- Align fork origin point to T.
- Complete lower section of seat seam.
- Mark start of inside leg seam.

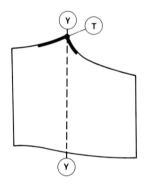

Fig. 23.6.

Stage 3:   Remain on Y axis (Fig. 23.7).
- Align side origin point to H.
- Mark hip section of side seam.

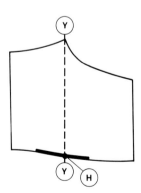

Fig. 23.7.

Stage 4:   Align Y axis of pattern to D axis on paper (Fig. 23.8).
- Align side origin point to H.
- Complete lower section of side seam.
- Mark part of hem.

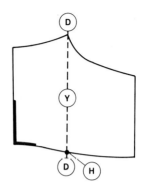

Fig. 23.8.

Stage 5:   Remain on D axis (Fig. 23.9).
- Align fork origin point to T.
- Complete inside leg seam and hem.

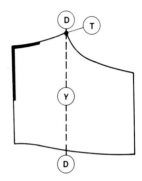

Fig. 23.9.

Stage 6:   Align X axes of pattern and paper (Fig. 23.10).
- Align Y axis of pattern to C axis on paper.
- Mark top section of seat seam.
- Mark part of yoke seam.

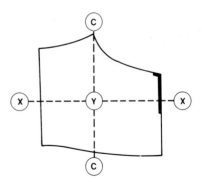

Fig. 23.10.

Stage 7: Remain on C axis (Fig. 23.11).
- Align side origin point to H.
- Complete side seam.
- Complete yoke seam.

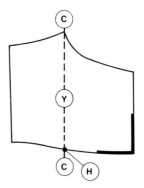

Fig. 23.11.

Stage 8: Use pattern to blend the seat seam (Fig. 23.12).

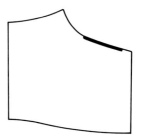

Fig. 23.12.

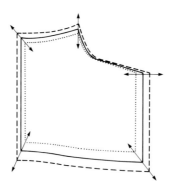

Fig. 23.13.

Grading instructions:
BACK YOKE

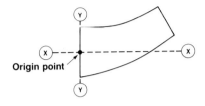

Fig. 23.14. Grading axes for yoke.

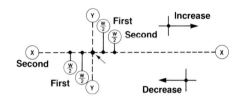

Fig. 23.15. Increment net.

Stage 1: Align X and Y axes of pattern and paper (Fig. 23.16).
- Mark CB.
- Mark start of waist seam.
- Mark start of yoke seam.

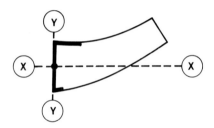

Fig. 23.16.

Stage 2: Remain on X axis (Fig. 23.17).
- Align origin point to first $\frac{W}{2}$.
- Mark central section of yoke.

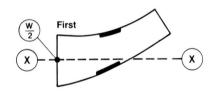

Fig. 23.17.

Stage 3: Remain on X axis (Fig. 23.18).
- Align origin point to second $\frac{W}{2}$.
- Mark side section of yoke.

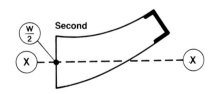

Fig. 23.18.

Stage 4:   Use pattern to blend the waist and yoke lines
(Fig. 23.19).

Fig. 23.19.

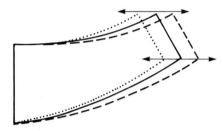

Fig. 23.20. Grade for yoke.

Grading instructions:
FRONT PANEL

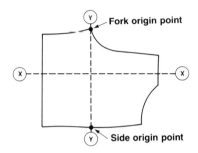

Fig. 23.21. Grading axes for front panel.

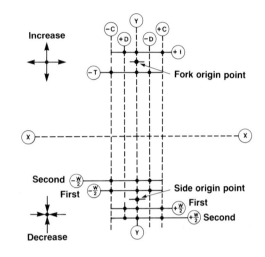

Fig. 23.22. Increment net.

Stage 1: Align X and Y axes of pattern and paper (Fig. 23.23).
- Mark part of lower section of fly seam.

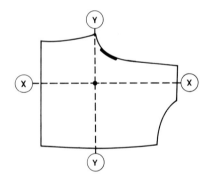

Fig. 23.23.

Stage 2: Remain on Y axis (Fig. 23.24).
- Align fork origin point to T.
- Complete lower section of fly seam.
- Mark start of inside leg seam.

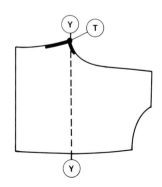

Fig. 23.24.

Stage 3: Remain on Y axis (Fig. 23.25).

- Align side origin point to second $\frac{W}{2}$.
- Mark hip section of side seam.

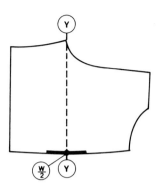

Fig. 23.25.

Stage 4: Align Y axis of pattern to D axis on paper (Fig. 23.26).

- Align side origin point to second $\frac{W}{2}$.
- Complete lower section of side seam.
- Mark part of hem.

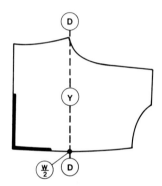

Fig. 23.26.

Stage 5: Remain on D axis (Fig. 23.27).
- Align fork origin point to T.
- Complete inside leg seam and hem.

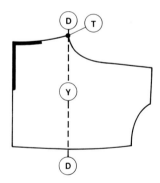

Fig. 23.27.

Stage 6: Align X axes of pattern and paper (Fig. 23.28).
- Align Y axis of pattern to C axis on paper.
- Mark top section of fly seam.
- Mark start of waist seam.

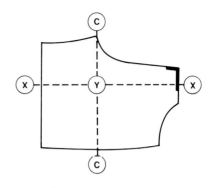

Fig. 23.28.

Stage 7: Remain on C axis (Fig. 23.29).
- Align side origin point to first $\frac{W}{2}$.
- Complete first part of waist seam.
- Mark part of pocket line.

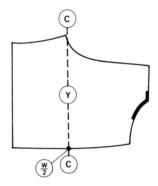

Fig. 23.29.

Stage 8: Remain on C axis (Fig. 23.30).
- Align side origin point to second $\frac{W}{2}$.
- Complete pocket line.
- Complete side seam.

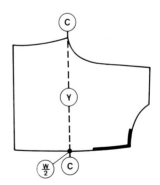

Fig. 23.30.

Stage 9: Use pattern to blend the fly seam (Fig. 23.31).

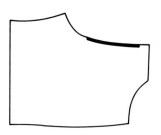

Fig. 23.31.

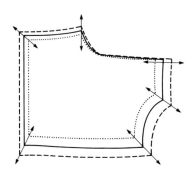

Fig. 23.32. Grade for front panel.

Grading instructions:
POCKET BAG

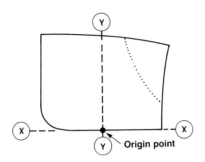

Fig. 23.33. Grading axes for pocket bag.

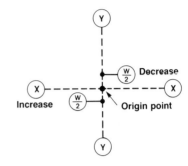

Fig. 23.34. Increment net.

Stage 1: Align X and Y axis of pattern and paper (Fig. 23.35).
- Mark side seam and nip.
- Mark part of waist line and part of pocket bottom.

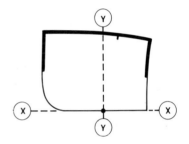

Fig. 23.35.

Stage 2: Remain on Y axis (Fig. 23.36).
- Align origin point to $\dfrac{W}{2}$.
- Complete pocket bag and mark waist nip.

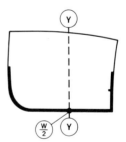

Fig. 23.36.

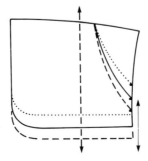

Fig. 23.37. Grade for pocket bag.

PART 5

COMPUTERISED GRADING TECHNOLOGY AND APPENDICES

Chapter 24

Computerised Grading

During the past twenty years or so, computerised pattern grading systems have become a widely used tool in the clothing industry, and at the time of writing there are over 6000 systems in operation throughout the world. The systems themselves perform a number of functions apart from pattern grading. These include:

- Pattern design: For the construction and development of garment patterns.
- Pattern generation: This program automatically generates patterns for secondary materials such as lining and fusibles, directly from the top cloth patterns.
- Cut and marker planning: A technique which determines the most viable method of cutting production orders.
- Marker planning: Producing cutting markers interactively or automatically to be used for manual or computerised cutting.

Most systems also have a number of specialised functions which provide management information for the planning and control of many administrative and production activities in a clothing factory.

Information flow

Computerised pattern grading is graphic data processing applied to the grading of garment patterns, and like all data processing it has three phases.

PHASE 1: DATA COLLECTION

This is the input phase and like manual grading it starts with all the components for the pattern which is to be graded. This master pattern is inputted to the computer by digitising or scanning; this is the process whereby each component is converted to an alphanumeric format which the computer can understand and process. During this phase data is also input to instruct the computer in precise terms what it is expected to accomplish. This information includes:

- The range of sizes required.
- The grading points of the pattern components.

Fig. 24.1. Graded nest of patterns.

- The grade rules which are to be applied to these points.
- The output form of the graded patterns.

The accuracy of the data inputted during this phase determines, in absolute terms, the accuracy of the output.

PHASE 2: DATA PROCESSING

This is the stage where all the grading procedures are performed by the system. Many manual grading techniques which require great skill and expertise on the part of the pattern grader become routine, simple elements when carried out on a computerised system. The results can be verified on a screen or by plotting them out on a miniature or full sized drawing. If necessary, alterations and modifications can be made at this stage before producing the finished set of patterns.

PHASE 3: DATA PRESENTATION

The last phase generates the graded patterns in the form requested at the input stage. This form can be:

- Nested grades (Fig. 24.1) drawn out by the plotter.
- Individual components cut out and notched in regular pattern paper.
- Mini scale nests or cut out patterns.

Fig. 24.2. Computerised system.

Where the graded patterns are to be used for planning cutting markers on the system, there is no need to generate patterns in any form other than that required for control purposes.

These three phases convert a master pattern into a range of graded sizes for further use.

System description

A typical system (Fig. 24.2) usually consists of five hardware units:

CENTRAL PROCESSING UNIT (Fig. 24.3)

This is the brain of the system and irrespective of how many different units there are in the system's configuration, the CPU is the centre of all activities. Any unit in the system which has electronic communication with the CPU is referred to as an on-line unit.

DISK UNIT

This unit includes the magnetic disc which is a mass storage device with real time recall, and it interfaces

directly with the CPU. The disk unit primarily provides data storage for on-going operations and information can be transferred from the disk to tapes or floppy disks for temporary or permanent storage.

VISUAL DISPLAY UNIT (Fig. 24.4)

The VDU is the basic work station of the system and provides the means to implement and visually monitor the functions of the system. The unit itself generally consists of:

- The screen that displays the work in progress.
- A keyboard which interfaces with the CPU and enables the operator to input commands.
- The data tablet and pen which are used for manipulatory routines and positioning patterns. These operations can also be performed by a device called a 'mouse' which also has function buttons.
- The work station can also have an on-line printer which prints out data, commands and system responses.

THE DIGITISER (Fig. 24.5)

This unit consists of a large plastic-covered work table and a free-floating cursor which converts the peripheral

Fig. 24.3. Central processing unit.

Fig. 24.4. Visual display unit (VDU).

Fig. 24.5. Digitiser.

Fig. 24.6. Free floating cursor.

and internal lines of a pattern component into a format understood by the system. This format is a description of these lines according to sets of X and Y co-ordinates from an origin point.

Under the plastic surface of the digitiser is a fine electronic network, similar to graph paper, which provides a high resolution grid for identifying any position on the table's surface. The cursor (Fig. 24.6) has two hair lines engraved on to the viewing glass and when the intersection of these two lines is placed on a pattern line and the correct button pressed, the location of that point is inputted to the system. This process is repeated around the pattern and along the internals such as pocket positions, darts etc. The cursor is also used to input grading instructions and other information which has positional characteristics on the pattern, such as notches and drill holes.

Another method of inputting patterns is by an electronic photo cell scanner (Fig. 24.7) which registers the outlines and cut-out internals of a pattern component. While scanning eliminates point-by-point digitising, grading and other information still has to be entered at the regular work station.

THE PLOTTER (Fig. 24.8)

This unit generates the grading output in the form of drawings or cut-out patterns and the actual cutting out of patterns can be performed by a knife attachment or a laser cutter. Most plotters are equipped with a display terminal which controls the work flow and the form of the output required.

While the systems on the market can vary in their hardware, operational procedures and programs, they all perform the same basic functions and there are systems at prices viable for nearly every size of factory.

The pattern grading process

The entire process of pattern grading by computer is based on co-ordinate rules which define the movements of the internal and external points of a pattern in order to increase or decrease its size. These are called grading rules and the movement is defined by allotting values to a point's movements in terms of X and Y.

A pattern component has two types of points which move during grading: grade points and secondary points.

GRADE POINTS

These are the points which have grading rules applied to them, and their positions in most cases are relative to the basic construction lines of the pattern.

SECONDARY POINTS

Sometimes called intermediate points, these lie between the grade points and move in accordance with

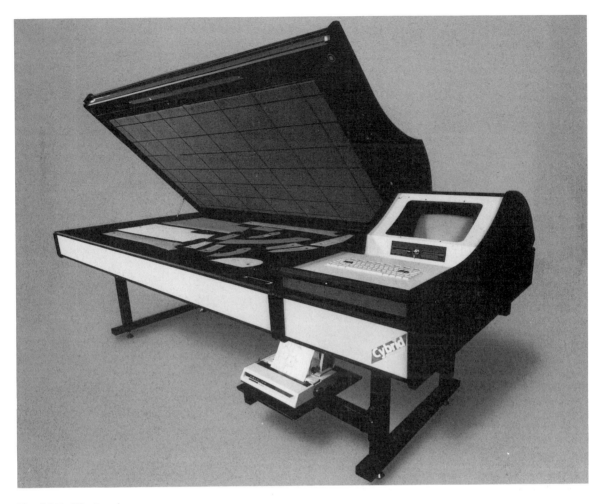

Fig. 24.7. Electronic scanner.

them. Fig. 24.9 shows a basic block pattern for a body garment front and illustrates the positions of the grading and secondary points in relation to the construction lines of the pattern. Straight lines only need the start and finish points, but acute curves require very closely spaced points. The points themselves are entered in a clockwise direction starting from the bottom left hand corner of the pattern component.

The definitions of movement of the grading points are based on an X and/or Y value relative to their origin point; there are a number of possibilities depending on the direction in which a point has to be moved. The movement grid is formed by X and Y axes which intersect each other at right angles; the intersection is the origin point O. Each of the axes has a plus or minus direction in relation to O and these are (Fig. 24.10):

X Axis: to the right of O = plus
         to the left of O = minus
Y Axis: above O = plus
         below O = minus

Thus a point can move in any one of eight directions relative to its origin. These movements are illustrated in Fig. 24.11.

A simple example of the compilation and effect of grade rules is shown in Fig. 24.12 where the grade from size to size is:

- Neck to waist: 5 mm.
- Back neck base width: 2.5 mm.
- Shoulder length: 2.5 mm.

Each rule relates to the position of a point when preceding movements have been completed, so

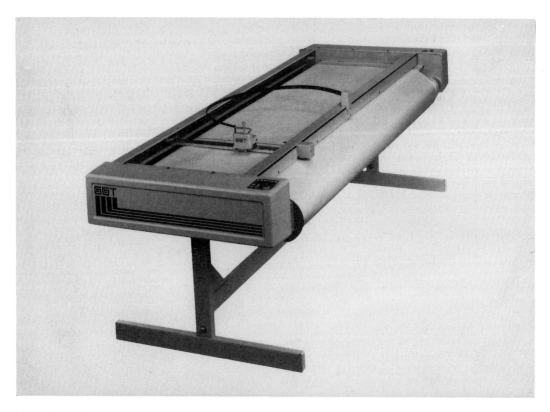

Fig. 24.8. Flatbed plotter.

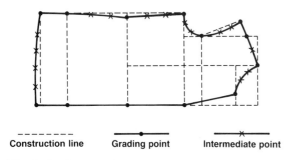

Construction line ---- Grading point ● Intermediate point ✕

Fig. 24.9. Construction lines and grading points.

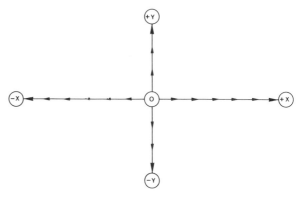

Fig. 24.10. The axes of movement.

although point 3 in the example actually moves a total of 5 mm in the Y direction, in practice it has only moved 2.5 mm following the grade movement for point 2. If the size intervals are the same for the larger and smaller sizes which are to be graded from the base size pattern, then only the values for a one-size up-grade have to be entered. The system automatically applies the one size rules when increasing size and reverses them for decreasing size.

Grading rules are stored in a grade rule library, each having a unique code symbol. When used the rule code is entered rather than the directional definitions and values of the rule. A rule can be applied to any point on any garment as long as the values and directions are suitable for that particular grade. Systems also have the capability for compiling new grade rules from existing

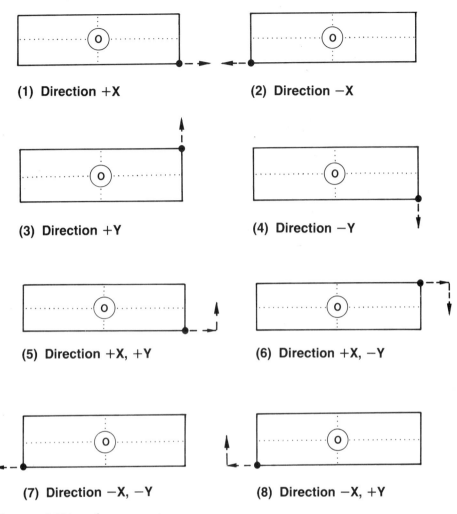

(1) Direction +X

(2) Direction −X

(3) Direction +Y

(4) Direction −Y

(5) Direction +X, +Y

(6) Direction +X, −Y

(7) Direction −X, −Y

(8) Direction −X, +Y

Fig. 24.11. The possibilities of movement.

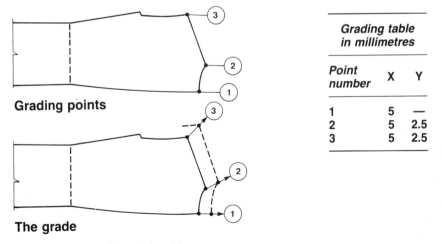

Grading points

The grade

Grading table in millimetres		
Point number	X	Y
1	5	—
2	5	2.5
3	5	2.5

Fig. 24.12. Grade of back neck and shoulder.

ones by taking, say, the X value from one rule and the Y value from another, and also for changing directions from plus to minus or vice versa. The grades of garments stored in the model file of the system are easily transferred to another garment without point by point entry.

A recent development in computerised pattern grading is a dynamic automatic grading system which automatically performs nearly all the functions concerned with the locations of grading points, and the calculation and application of grading rules for even the most complex patterns. This revolutionary new concept is based on two main principles:

(1) The grading rules are calculated directly from the size chart input to the system. The rules for these calculations can be those of the user or standard ones.

(2) There is a direct relationship between the grade of a block pattern and that for a styled pattern developed from it.

Although this technology is very new, it points to the direction which computerised grading technology will take in the future.

TO SUM UP

Irrespective of the technology used to grade patterns, the final results will only be as good as the grading system itself. A primitive and poorly formulated system will remain that way however much it is computerised.

Chapter 25

Size Charts

The size charts appearing in the following pages come from a variety of sources and where possible these are acknowledged. I extend my thanks to the organisations and publishers who gave me permission to reproduce their charts in this book.

Some charts came from clothing retailers and manufacturers who gave their permission to use them but asked for the sources not to be acknowledged. I respect their wishes and should like to thank them all for allowing me the opportunity to use these charts in order to show what the big guns of the menswear industry are doing as regards sizing. It is these size charts, more than any other, which were used as a basis for developing the grading system demonstrated in this book.

Size charts 1 to 8 are reproduced by permission of HAKA Treuhand GmbH, Cologne.

SIZE CHART NO. 1
OVERGARMENTS

Height group: Medium *Fitting*: Regular

					Size symbols			
No.	Measurement	44	46	48	50	52	54	56	58
1.	Chest girth	88	92	96	100	104	108	112	116
2.	Waist girth (trousers)	76	80	84	88	92	98	102	108
3.	Seat girth	96	100	104	108	112	116	119	122
10.	Across back	37	38	39	40	41	42	43	44
13.	Height	168	171	174	177	180	182	184	186
15.	Nape to waist	42	43	44	45	46	46.5	47	47.5
20.	Outside leg	98	100.5	103	104.5	106	107.5	109	110.5
21.	Inside leg	74	76	78	79	80	81	82	83
22.	Forearm length	43	44	45	46	47	47.5	48	48.5

Source: HAKA-Verbandes, Germany.

SIZE CHART NO. 2
OVERGARMENTS

Height group: Tall   *Fitting*: Regular

No.	Measurement	Size symbols					
		90	94	98	102	106	110
1.	Chest girth	88	92	96	100	104	108
2.	Waist girth (trousers)	76	80	84	88	92	96
3.	Seat girth	98	102	106	110	114	118
10.	Across back	37	38	39	40	41	42
13.	Height	177	180	183	186	188	190
15.	Nape to waist	45	46	47	48	48.5	49
20.	Outside leg	104	106	108	110	112	113
21.	Inside leg	79	80	81	82	83	84
22.	Forearm length	46	47	48	49	49.5	50

Source: HAKA-Verbandes, Germany.

SIZE CHART NO. 3
OVERGARMENTS

Height group: Medium   *Fitting*: Stocky

No.	Measurement	Size symbols							
		22	23	24	25	26	27	28	29
1.	Chest girth	88	92	96	100	104	108	112	116
2.	Waist girth (trousers)	80	84	88	92	96	100	106	110
3.	Seat girth	96	100	104	108	112	116	120	124
10.	Across back	37	38	39	40	41	42	43	44
13.	Height	162	165	168	171	174	176	178	180
15.	Nape to waist	41	42	43	44	44.5	45	45.5	46
20.	Outside leg	94	96.5	99	101.5	103	104.5	106	107.5
21.	Inside leg	70	72	74	76	77	78	79	80
22.	Forearm length	42	43	44	45	45.5	46	46.5	47

Source: HAKA-Verbandes, Germany.

SIZE CHART NO. 4
OVERGARMENTS

Height group: Short   Fitting: Stocky

No.	Measurement	Size symbols							
		225	235	245	255	265	275	285	295
1.	Chest girth	88	92	96	100	104	108	112	116
2.	Waist girth (trousers)	82	86	90	94	98	102	106	112
3.	Seat girth	98	102	106	110	114	118	122	126
10.	Across back	37	38	39	40	41	42	43	44
13.	Height	156	159	162	165	168	170	172	174
15.	Nape to waist	40	41	42	43	44.5	45	45.5	46
20.	Outside leg	90	92.5	95	96.5	98	99.5	101	102.5
21.	Inside leg	67	69	71	72	73	74	75	76
22.	Forearm length	41	42	43	44	44.5	45	45.5	46

Source: HAKA-Verbandes, Germany.

SIZE CHART NO. 5
OVERGARMENTS

Height group: Medium   Fitting: Large

No.	Measurement	Size symbols						
		144	146	148	150	152	154	156
1.	Chest girth	88	92	96	100	104	108	112
2.	Waist girth (trousers)	80	84	88	92	96	102	106
3.	Seat girth	98	102	106	110	114	118	122
10.	Across back	37	38	39	40	41	42	43
13.	Height	168	171	174	177	180	182	184
15.	Nape to waist	42	43	44	45	46	46.5	47
20.	Outside leg	98	100.5	103	104.5	106	107.5	109
21.	Inside leg	74	76	78	79	80	81	82
22.	Forearm length	43	44	45	46	47	47.5	48

Source: HAKA-Verbandes, Germany.

SIZE CHART NO. 6
OVERGARMENTS

Height group: Medium   *Fitting*: Athletic

No.	Measurement	Size symbols					
		440	460	480	500	520	540
1.	Chest girth	88	92	96	100	104	108
2.	Waist girth (trousers)	72	76	80	84	88	92
3.	Seat girth	92	96	100	104	108	112
10.	Across back	38	39	40	41	42	43
13.	Height	168	171	174	177	180	182
15.	Nape to waist	42	43	44	45	46	47
20.	Outside leg	98	100.5	103	104.5	106	107.5
21.	Inside leg	74	76	78	79	80	81
22.	Forearm length	43	44	45	46	47	47.5

Source: HAKA-Verbandes, Germany.

SIZE CHART NO. 7
OVERGARMENTS

Height group: Medium   *Fitting*: Corpulent

No.	Measurement	Size symbols					
		47	49	51	53	55	57	59
1.	Chest girth	92	96	100	104	108	112	116
2.	Waist girth (trousers)	96	100	104	110	114	120	124
3.	Seat girth	102	106	110	114	118	122	126
10.	Across back	39	40	41	42	43	44	45
13.	Height	166	168	170	172	174	176	178
15.	Nape to waist	42.5	43	43.5	44	44.5	45	45.5
20.	Outside leg	99	101	103	105	107	109	111
21.	Inside leg	72	73	74	75	76	77	78
22.	Forearm length	43.5	44	44.5	45	45.5	46	46.5

Source: HAKA-Verbandes, Germany.

SIZE CHART NO. 8
OVERGARMENTS

		Size symbols				
Height group: Short		*Fitting*: Corpulent				
No.	*Measurement*	495	515	535	555	575
1.	Chest girth	96	100	104	108	112
2.	Waist girth (trousers)	100	104	110	114	120
3.	Seat girth	106	110	114	118	122
10.	Across back	40	41	42	43	44
13.	Height	162	164	166	168	170
15.	Nape to waist	41.5	42	42.5	43	43.5
20.	Outside leg	96	98	100	102	104
21.	Inside leg	96	98	100	102	104
22.	Forearm length	42.5	43	43.5	44	44.5

Source: HAKA-Verbandes, Germany.

SIZE CHART NO. 9
OVERGARMENTS

		Size symbols					
Height group: Medium		*Fitting*: Regular					
No.	*Measurement*	36	38	40	42	44	46
1.	Chest girth	−2.5	−2.5	0	+2.5	+2.5	+2.5
2.	Waist girth (trousers)	−2.5	−2.5	0	+2.5	+2.5	+2.5
3.	Seat girth	−2.5	−2.5	0	+2.5	+2.5	+2.5
8.	Upper arm girth	−1.0	−1.0	0	+1.0	+1.0	+1.0
9.	Wrist girth	−0.8	−0.8	0	+0.8	+0.8	+0.8
10.	Across back (half)	−0.6	−0.6	0	+0.6	+0.6	+0.6
11.	Across chest	−1.3	−1.3	0	+1.3	+1.3	+1.3
12.	Shoulder length	−0.3	−0.3	0	+0.3	+0.3	+0.3
22.	Arm length	−1.0	−1.0	0	+1.0	+1.0	+1.0

Source: English retailer sourcing throughout the world.
This company provides its suppliers with size 40 block patterns from which they develop styled garments. The retailer's size chart provides size intervals for grading and not the measurements which are generally included in conventional size charts.

SIZE CHART NO. 10
TROUSERS

Height group: Medium   *Fitting*: Regular

		Size symbols							
No.	Measurement	28	30	32	34	36	38	40	42
2.	Waist girth	−2.5	−2.5	−2.5	0	+2.5	+2.5	+2.5	+2.5
3.	Seat girth	−2.5	−2.5	−2.5	0	+2.5	+2.5	+2.5	+2.5
5.	Thigh girth	−1.5	−1.5	−1.5	0	+1.5	+1.5	+1.5	+1.5
6.	Knee girth	−1.0	−1.0	−1.0	0	+1.0	+1.0	+1.0	+1.0
7.	Ankle girth	−1.0	−1.0	−1.0	0	+1.0	+1.0	+1.0	+1.0
17.	Waist to crotch line	−0.9	−0.9	−0.9	0	+0.9	+0.9	+0.9	+0.9
20.	Outside leg	−1.0	−1.0	−1.0	0	+1.0	+1.0	+1.0	+1.0
21.	Inside leg	0	0	0	0	0	0	0	0

Source: English retailer sourcing throughout the world.
This is the same company as that described in Chart No. 9 and they supply their manufacturers with a size 34 block pattern for trousers. The size chart above relates to the grading intervals for a particular style.

SIZE CHART NO. 11
TROUSERS

Height group: Medium   *Fitting*: Regular

		Size symbols							
No.	Measurement	28	30	32	34	36	38	40	42
2.	Waist girth	36.3	38.8	41.3	43.8	46.3	48.8	51.3	53.8
3.	Seat girth	51.5	53.5	55.5	57.5	59.5	61.5	63.5	65.5
5.	Thigh girth	28.2	29	29.8	30.6	31.4	31.2	32	32.8
6.	Knee girth	25	25.5	26	26.5	27	27.5	28	28.5
7.	Ankle girth	21	21.5	22	22.5	23	23.5	24	24.5
20.	Outside leg	103	103.6	104.2	104.8	105.4	106	106.8	107.4
21.	Inside leg	79	79	79	79	79	79	79	79

Source: English chain retailer.
This is a garment measurement chart with the girth measurements taken on half the leg or garment.

SIZE CHART NO. 12
TROUSERS

					Size symbols				
No.	*Measurement*	28	30	32	34	36	38	40	42
2.	Waist girth	36	38.5	41	43.5	46	48.5	51	53.5
3.	Seat girth	51	53	55	57	59	61.5	64	66.5
5.	Thigh girth	28.5	29.3	31.2	32.1	33	33.9	34.8	35.7
6.	Knee girth	26	26.5	27	27.5	28	28.5	29	29.5
7.	Ankle girth	21.5	22	22.5	23	23.5	24	24.5	25
20.	Outside leg	99.7	100.6	101.5	102.4	103.3	104.2	105.1	106
21.	Inside leg	75	75	75	75	75	75	75	75

Height group: Short   *Fitting*: Regular

Source: English retailer.
This is a garment measurement chart with the girths being measured on half the garment or leg.

SIZE CHART NO. 13
JACKETS

Height group: Medium   *Fitting*: Regular

				Size symbols			
No.	*Measurement*	36	38	40	42	44	46
1.	Chest girth	−25	−25	0	+25	+25	+25
2.	Waist girth	−25	−25	0	+25	+25	+25
3.	Seat girth	−25	−25	0	+25	+25	+25
8.	Upper arm girth	−10	−10	0	+10	+10	+10
9.	Wrist girth	−8	−8	0	+8	+8	+8
11.	Across chest	−9	−9	0	+9	+9	+9
12.	Shoulder length	−3	−3	0	+3	+3	+3
15.	Nape to waist	−5	−5	0	+5	+5	+5
16.	Jacket length	−10	−10	0	+10	+10	+10
22.	Arm length	−12	−12	0	+12	+12	+12

Source: English manufacturer.
This is a grading chart from a base size 40 used for the English home market.

SIZE CHART NO. 14
TROUSERS

Height group: As chart			*Fitting*:				
				Size symbols			
Measurement	28	30	32	34	36	38	40	42
Short: inside leg	73	73	73	73	73	73	73	73
Short: outside leg	99	99.8	100.6	101.4	102.2	103	103.8	104.6
Medium: inside leg	78	78	78	78	78	78	78	78
Medium: outside leg	104	104.8	105.6	106.4	107.2	108	108.8	109.6
Long: inside leg	88	88	88	88	88	88	88	88
Long: outside leg	110.5	111.3	112.1	112.9	113.7	114.5	115.3	116.1
Extra long: inside leg	93	93	93	93	93	93	93	93
Extra long: outside leg	116	116.8	117.6	118.4	119.2	120	120.8	121.6

Source: English retailer.

This is an extract from a retailer's size chart and shows the trouser lengths used for each of the four height groups catered for.

SIZE CHART NO. 15
JACKETS

Height group: Medium			*Fitting*: Regular					
					Size symbols			
No.	*Measurement*	44	46	48	50	52	54	56	58
1.	Chest girth	88	92	96	100	104	108	112	116
2.	Waist girth	76	80	84	88	92	97	102	107
3.	Seat girth	95	99	103	107	111	115	118	121
9.	Wrist girth	30	31	32	33	34	35	36	37
10.	Across back	45	46	47	48	49	50	51	52
12.	Shoulder length	15.5	15.75	16.0	16.25	16.5	16.75	17	17.25
16.	Jacket length	73	74	75	76	77	78	79	80
22.	Arm length	60.5	61.5	62.5	63.5	64.5	65.5	66.5	67.5

Source: German retailer.

SIZE CHART NO. 16
TROUSERS

Height group: Medium   *Fitting*: Regular

No.	Measurement	38	40	42	44	46	48
				Size symbols			
2.	Waist girth	37	39	41	43	45	47
3.	Seat girth	52	54	56	58	60	62
6.	Knee girth	27	27.7	28.2	28.7	29.2	29.7
7.	Ankle girth	21.8	21.8	22.5	22.5	22.9	23.2
20.	Outside leg	106	107.5	109	110.5	112.5	114
21.	Inside leg	78	79	80	81	83	84

Source: German retailer.

SIZE CHART NO. 17
JACKETS

Height group: Medium   *Fitting*: Regular

No.	Measurement	44	46	48	50	52	54	56	58
					Size symbols				
1.	Chest girth	110	113.4	116.8	120.2	123.6	127	130.4	133.8
2.	Waist girth	94.4	98.4	102.4	106.4	110.4	114.4	118.4	122.4
10.	Across back	42.6	43.6	44.6	45.6	46.6	47.6	48.6	49.6
12.	Shoulder length	15.1	15.4	15.7	16	16.3	16.6	16.9	17.2
22.	Arm length	60.6	61.8	63	64.2	65.4	66.6	67.6	68.6
23.	Jacket length	72.5	74	75.5	77	78.5	80	81	82

Source: Dutch retailer.
This is a somewhat hybrid type of size chart, but it evidently works well enough for this particular retailer.

SIZE CHART NO. 18
JACKETS

Height group: Medium   *Fitting*: Regular

No.	Measurement	Size symbols					
		36	38	40	42	44	46
1.	Chest girth	91	96	101	106	111	116
2.	Waist girth	81	86	91	96	101	106
3.	Seat girth	101	106	111	116	121	126
8.	Upper arm girth	40	41.2	42.4	43.6	44.8	46
9.	Wrist girth	30	31.2	32.2	33.2	34.2	35.2
11.	Across chest	25.1	26	26.9	27.8	28.7	29.6
12.	Shoulder length	15.8	16.1	16.4	16.7	17	17.3
16.	Jacket length	75	76.2	77.4	78.6	79.8	81
22.	Arm length	61.4	62.6	63.8	65.2	66.4	67.6

Source: American retailer.

SIZE CHART NO. 19
OVERGARMENTS, TROUSERS AND CASUAL WEAR

Height group:
170 cm – 178 cm   *Fitting*: Regular – mature

No.	Measurement	Not given								
		44	46	48	50	52	54	56	58	
1.	Chest girth	88	92	96	100	104	108	112	116	120
2.	Waist girth	74	78	82	86	90	98	102	106	110
3.	Seat girth	92	96	100	104	108	114	118	122	126
4.	Neck size	37	38	39	40	41	42	43	44	45
9.	Wrist girth (close)	16.4	16.8	17.2	17.6	18	18.4	18.8	19.2	19.6
17.	Body rise	26.8	27.2	27.6	28	28.4	28.8	29.2	29.6	30
21.	Inside leg	78	79	80	81	82	82	82	82	82
22.	Sleeve length	63.6	64.2	64.8	65.4	66	66	66	66	66

Source: *Metric Pattern Cutting for Menswear* by Winifred Aldrich.
Reproduced by permission of Blackwell Scientific Publications, Osney Mead, Oxford, England.

SIZE CHART NO. 20
OVERGARMENTS AND TROUSERS

Height group: Medium   *Fitting*: Regular

| | | | | | Size symbols | | | |
| | | | | | Not given | | | |
No.	Measurement								
1.	Chest girth	86.5	91.5	96.5	101.5	106.5	111.5	116.5	121.5
2.	Waist girth	71.5	76.5	81.5	86.5	91.5	96.5	101.5	106.5
3.	Seat girth	91.5	96.5	101.5	106.5	111.5	116.5	121.5	126.5
4.	Neck base girth	35.5	37	38	39.5	40.5	42	43	44.5
6.	Knee girth	49.5	50.5	52	53	54.5	56	57	58.5
7.	Ankle girth	46	47	48.5	49.5	50.5	52	53.5	54.5
10.	Across back	40.5	41	42	42.5	43	44	44.5	45
13.	Height	168	173	178	183	188	193	198	203
15.	Nape to waist	42	43	44.5	45.5	47	49.5	49.5	50.5
17.	Waist to crotch line	27	27.5	28.5	30	30.5	32	32.5	33.5
20.	Outside leg	101.5	108	114	120.5	127	133	139.5	146
21.	Inside leg	75	80.5	86.5	91	96.5	102	107	112.5
22.	Forearm length	43	44.5	45.5	47	48.5	49.5	50.5	52

Source: *The Art of Grading Patterns* by Alice Defty.
Reproduced by permission of Butterworths, Durban, South Africa.

SIZE CHART NO. 21
OVERGARMENTS

Height group:
Medium-dynamic   *Fitting*: Regular – mature

| | | | | | Size symbols | | | |
No.	Measurement	44	46	48	50	52	54	56	58
1.	Chest girth	88	92	96	100	104	108	112	116
2.	Waist girth	76	80	84	88	92	98	102	108
3.	Seat girth	96	100	104	108	112	116	119	122
10.	Across back	37	38	39	40	41	42	43	44
15.	Nape to waist	42	43	44	45	46	46.5	47	47.5

Source: German manufacturer of garment stands.
Reproduced by permission of Berliner Buestenfabrik GmbH, Berlin, Germany.

SIZE CHART NO. 22
OVERGARMENTS

No.	Measurement	*Height group: —*			*Fitting*: Regular			
		Size symbols						
		34	36	38	40	42	44	46
1.	Chest girth	86.5	91.5	96.5	101.5	106.5	111.5	116.5
2.	Waist girth	74	79	84	89	94	99	104
3.	Seat girth	91.5	96.5	101.5	106.5	111.5	116.5	121.5

(Measurements for Model GB)
Source: English manufacturer of garment stands.
Reproduced by permission of Kennett and Lindsell Ltd, Romford, England.

Glossary of Technical Terms and Abbreviations

Anterior   To the front.

Block pattern   A template of a basic pattern form on which styling details can be superimposed.

Button stand   The distance from the centre of a button to the edge of the garment.

CB   Centre back.

Cervical   The seventh of the cervical vertebrae.

CF   Centre front.

Distal   Belonging to the back, directed backwards.

Fork   The point at which the legs of a pair of trousers are joined.

Gorge   The neckline of the front to which the collar is joined.

Grading   A technique for re-constructing a garment pattern in a different size.

Lapel break   The lower end of the lapel which is usually a small distance above the highest or first buttonhole.

Scye   Another word for the armhole of a garment.

Sleeve head vertex   The uppermost point of the sleeve head.

Topside   The front panel of a trouser leg.

Underside   The back panel of a trouser leg.

Bibliography

(1) Alcega, Juan de (1589) *Tailors Pattern Book*. Republished 1979, Ruth Bean, Bedford, England.

(2) Aldrich, W. (1989) *Metric Pattern Cutting for Menswear*. Blackwell Scientific Publications, Oxford, England.

(3) Beever, H. (Ed.) (No date) *Clothing Terms and Definitions*. The Clothing Institute, London, England.

(4) Bulsara, R.N. (1981) *The Art and Science of Designing, Drafting, Grading and Cutting Men's Garments*. V-Design Publications, London, England.

(5) Croney, J. (1980) *Anthropometry for Designers*. Batsford Academic and Educational Ltd, London, England.

(6) Defty, A. (1984) *The Art of Grading Patterns*. Butterworths, Durban, South Africa.

(7) Dreyfuss, H. (1978) *The Measure of Man*. Bobbin Publications, South Carolina, USA.

(8) Fuller, E. and Clark, S. (No date) *Pattern Grading*. Tailor and Cutter, London, England.

(9) Gioello, D.A. and Berke, B. (1979) *Figure Types and Size Ranges*. Fairchild Publications, New York, USA.

(10) Handford, J. (1980) *Professional Pattern Grading for Women's, Men's and Children's Apparel*. Plycon Press, California, USA.

(11) Le Merrer, J.V. (No date) *Methode de Gradation pour Hommes et Garconets*. Editions Vaudair S.A.R.L., Paris, France.

(12) Master Designer (1983) *Modern Garment Design and Grading*. Master Designer Inc., Chicago, USA.

(13) Muller, M. (No date) *Vergrossern und Verkleinerin fur Herrenbekleidung*. Deutsche Bekleidungs Akademie, Munich, Germany.

(14) Poole, B.W. (1927) *The Science of Pattern Construction for Garment Makers*. New Era Publishing, London, England.

(15) Sheldon, S. and Baker, M. (1940) *The Varieties of Human Physique*. Harpers, New York, USA.

(16) Taylor, P.J. and Shoben, M.M. (1990) *Grading for the Fashion Industry*. Stanley Thornes (Publishers), Cheltenham, England.